CREATING CHRISTIAN PERSONALITY

By A. Don Augsburger

HERALD PRESS
Scottdale, Pa.

CREATING CHRISTIAN PERSONALITY

*Dedicated
in Loving Response
to My Parents
Who Provided a Wholesome Atmosphere
for My Early Years of Nurture*

THE CONRAD GREBEL LECTURES

The Conrad Grebel Lectureship was set up in 1950 for the purpose of making possible an annual study by a Mennonite scholar of some topic of interest and value to the Mennonite Church and to other Christian people. It is administered by the Conrad Grebel Lectureship Committee appointed by and responsible to the Mennonite Board of Education. The committee appoints the lecturers, approves their subjects, counsels them during their studies, and arranges for the delivery of the lectures at one or more places.

The lectureship is financed by donors who contribute annually $500 each.

Conrad Grebel was an influential leader in the sixteenth-century Swiss Anabaptist movement and is honored as one of the founders of the Mennonite Church.

The lectures are published by Herald Press, Scottdale, Pa. 15683, as soon as feasible after the delivery of the lectures. The date of publication by Herald Press is indicated by parenthesis.

Lectures thus far delivered are as follows:

1952 — Foundations of Christian Education, by Paul Mininger.

1953 — The Challenge of Christian Stewardship (1955), by Milo Kauffman.

1954 — The Way of the Cross in Human Relations (1958), by Guy F. Hershberger.

1955 — The Alpha and the Omega (1955), by Paul Erb.

1956 — The Nurture and Evangelism of Children (1959), by Gideon G. Yoder.

1957 — The Holy Spirit and the Holy Life (1959), by Chester K. Lehman.

1959 — The Church Apostolic (1960), by J. D. Graber.

1960 — These Are My People (1962), by Harold S. Bender.

1963 — Servant of God's Servants (1964), by Paul M. Miller.

1964 — The Resurrected Life (1965), by John R. Mumaw.

1965 — Creating Christian Personality (1966), by A. Don Augsburger.

1966 — God's Word Written (1966), by J. C. Wenger.

1967 — The Christian and Revolution (1968), by Melvin Gingerich.
1968-1969 — The Discerning Community — Church Renewal, by J. Lawrence Burkholder.
1970 — Woman Liberated (1971), by Lois Gunden Clemens.
1973 — In Praise of Leisure (1974), by Harold D. Lehman.

INTRODUCTION

Human personality is God's most valuable creation. Its complexity and potential are tremendous. The factors which bring about positive change in human behavior are many and varied. Today there are numerous voices speaking about youth nurture. The pressures bearing upon youth and parents are large. Cultural and geographic isolation no longer protects against the onslaught of the world. The problem is not only to stand up under the pressures of today but also to live effective, productive lives in the midst of these pressures. Concern for this problem led the General Council of the Mennonite Church to authorize a thorough interdisciplinary study of Mennonite youth and to assign responsibility for the study to the Mennonite Commission for Christian Education. The Commission appointed the Christian Nurture Study Committee to give overall direction to the study. A. Don Augsburger's research on home and church patterns of control and their influence on college freshmen was one of the important research studies carried out.

What is the result of the total study? Can research really help us evaluate the nature of our situation, help us understand the dynamics at work, and help us strengthen the nurture program? These are difficult questions. There are no easy and simple answers. Pious exhortation is not enough. There is no gimmick, pill, or procedure which will solve our problem. There are obvious limitations to this study. Human personality and God's Spirit are not easily compressed into research dimensions. Certain areas were not fully studied. The research study, however, found some recurring themes. In view of the great need for helpful Christian nurture materials today and the availability of the significant research data of this study, the Mennonite Commission for Christian Education and the Christian Nurture Study Committee recommended that a Conrad Grebel lecture be given in this area. The Conrad Grebel Lectureship Committee asked A. Don Augsburger to prepare this series of lectures.

His book, *Creating Christian Personality*, utilizes the basic research of the study, projects an approach to Christian nurture, and makes many practical suggestions to parents, pastors, and youth workers. The book emphasizes (1) the need for mutual respect and understanding between youth, parents, and pastors, (2) the crucial importance of a personal Christian experience, (3) the significance of a climate of affection and mutual caring in the home and in the church, (4) the importance of consistency of control in dealing with youth, and (5) the value of openness, integrity, forgiveness, and reconciliation in all of the fabric of relationships of family and church. Faith, hope, expectancy, and aspiration are recognized as strong motivating forces. Sharp judgmental, harsh, and self-righteous attitudes are not conducive to the transference of healthy attitudes and desirable church beliefs and practices to youth. Neither an extreme authoritarian nor an extreme permissive climate is desirable for Christian nurture. Reasonable structure and order emerging out of a deep sense of caring and mutual respect in the family and church and consistency in control patterns contribute most toward the development of productive, effective witnesses in the contemporary world. *Creating Christian Personality* will be helpful to parents, teachers, pastors, and youth workers. The book lends itself to use in study groups. Its contribution to the literature in this field is a very substantial one. The application of Christian caring to every fabric of human relationship, the central theme of the book, is the high test for all who take seriously their Christian commitment.

Atlee Beechy, Chairman
Christian Nurture Study Committee

PREFACE

It is the intention of these chapters to deal rather carefully with the developmental problems of the adolescent. It is not intended that the parents be omitted, however, for they are most essential in this process. An attempt will be made to relate both parental and church responsibility to the response of the developing youth. It should be understood that the major focus in the nurture process will be upon the role of the parents. This does not mean that the church and community are not responsible. It is simply to say that *the home is the basic unit in society for the development of Christian persons.* The church is a fellowship of families under God for the extension of Christian nurture.

The direction for these discussions grew out of the work and concern of the Christian Nurture Study Committee, a committee formed by the General Council of General Conference, and the Mennonite Commission for Christian Education. The impetus for a study dealing with youth of the Mennonite Church and their problems came from a number of sources.

Concern has been raised about a "disturbing lack of sense of mission and of direction among I-W men." This condition seems to be a result of the lack of spiritual vitality in the church in general. It is assumed that "Mennonites are failing frequently to develop maturity and personal responsibility in young people."

In a report by the Relief and Service Committee to the General Council of Mennonite General Conference the I-W situation was reviewed. The report expressed deep concern over the amount of deviant behavior by some I-W men and an apparent lack of incentive for witness by a somewhat larger group. The report prompted a serious and an extensive study of the situation. The concerns of this meeting are apparent in the following statement presented at that time by the Relief and Service Committee.

In view of the implications of the behavior patterns and attitudes of a sizable number of I-W men and indications which come from other areas of our church life that these attitudes are problems to many of our youth including our girls and young women in other situations, we urge the General Council to set up a broad study which would direct its energy toward better understanding of our youth, evaluating our church patterns and concerns in the light of these understandings, seeking Biblical clarification for further direction toward any pitfalls, and provide for getting this information out to conferences, pastors, and parents and into our general representatives, General Conference Christian education officers, Bible scholars, youth representatives, representatives of student personnel offices from our colleges and seminaries, and professional personnel from the field of medicine or psychiatry, psychology, and social work. An *ad hoc* committee working for two to four years might complete a study, prepare a guidance manual for pastors and parents, and make someone available on the basis similar to the Conrad Grebel Lectures for personal interpretation to churches, conferences, and ministers' meetings.

Mennonite colleges and other schools also expressed interest in a thorough study dealing with the behavior and witness pattern of youth.

The General Council approved the recommendation and asked the Mennonite Commission for Christian Education to become responsible for implementing the study. The Commission for Christian Education accepted the assignment and set up a committee composed of Atlee Beechy, Eldon King, Paul Lederach, and C. K. Lehman. It was the task of this committee to begin work, outlining scope and tentative plans and procedures for the study. This committee reported to the Commission for Christian Education and they appointed a Christian Nurture Study Committee composed of Ray Bair, Richard Detweiler, Eugene Herr, Howard Kauffman, Paul Lederach, Norman Loux, Boyd Nelson, J. C. Wenger, and A. Don Augsburger. Anna Mae Charles and Mrs. Marianna Stutzman were appointed to the committee later. Arnold Cressman became a member of the committee when he assumed his duties as Field Worker for the Commission for Christian Education. Ray Bair requested release from the committee when his services with the Commission terminated. Atlee Beechy, as chairman of the committee, gave direction for a careful and scholarly study of the area of concern.

Under the direction of the committee a number of individuals were given specific assignments in research related to various phases of the study.

The ultimate objective of the total study was "to secure facts, insights, and understandings which can be used in a more vital and effective nurturing of our youth in the church and result in a more dynamic total church and family life and witness to the world."

The research problems were divided into three phases:

1. To identify those attitudes and behavior patterns which indicate the degree to which a person approximates an "ideal Christian youth," or image of what youth should be like. For research purposes, this primarily necessitated the construction of some type of scale designed to rate the attitudes and / or behavior of specific persons. Those then that rated high on the scale were those who approached the attitudes and behavior of an "ideal Christian youth," and those who rated low were regarded as deviant.

2. To discover, for a given sample of youth, which persons rated higher and which lower on the scale of attitudes and behavior. This involved the step of actually administering a questionnaire to a sample of youth.

3. To compare those who were high on the scale with those who rated low, in order to see what important "causes" seem to explain the difference in ratings between the "highs" and the "lows."

The committee, following the objective and various phases of the study as outlined, met numerous times to give thought concerning and direction to the research in process by those asked to undertake specific aspects of the study.

At a later date the committee, researchers, and invited participants met at the Laurelville Camp in a four-day workshop for the purpose of reviewing research and drawing up recommendations. One of the recommendations for meeting the apparent need relative to the area of Christian nurture was the securing of an individual to bring together the findings of the researchers and the committee into lectures to be given throughout the church for the purpose of stimulating thought and discussion concerning the problems and basic issues in relation to Christian nurture. The following chapters are an attempt to do this.

In these chapters an attempt is made to delineate the problems, point out the areas of responsibility, and propose expectations in relation to the challenge of Christian nurture.

The writer wishes to thank both the Christian Nurture Study Committee and those who made the research materials available as well as both the General Council of General Conference and the Conrad Grebel Lectureship Committee for making it possible to pursue a study which has proved to be of measureless value to him. It is his desire also that through the grace of God and the competent leadership of the Holy Spirit, this material shall be of value to all who read these pages.

August 31, 1965   A. Don Augsburger

CONTENTS

1 DEVELOPMENT CAN BE PLANNED

Christian nurture doesn't just happen. It is the result of Christian relationships charged with careful planning and spiritual living. Character is formed as persons relate to each other. A son becomes like his father, or a daughter like her mother. The influence of associations is irresistible. Whether persons want to be changed or not may be of little significance. The patterns of other persons mold the lives of all of us. The individual, however, is responsible for what happens to him. You cannot make a person what he does not want to be, but you can create a desire to become. The forces of associations are so strong that they become the modeler of one's behavior. Youth may act like their friends to be accepted. The choice of these friends is an important decision.

Kind, loving personalities who live lives of meaning and usefulness are no accident. Appropriate behavior stems from Christian ideals which are the result of planned nurture. I do not mean closely regimented nurture that is so formal that persons become frustrated by living under a law of order and precision. I am referring to the kind of nurture that comes through Christian magnetism. This is the kind of living that begets true character. Planned environment provides opportunity for youth to see the true meaning of the Christian life. They may, in spite of proper nurture, become persons who resist Christian principles. The likelihood that they will reject Christian truth is certainly less where persons relate in true Christian experiences. Love and understanding acceptance for all family members regardless of sex, appearance, intelligence, or other factors are of supreme importance. When a person feels that he belongs to a Christian .group, it is more likely he will become a desirable Christian person. *Belonging in the home begets security and security begets openness to truth.*

NOT BY WORDS ALONE

Christianity is a language that must be lived to be read. Words! Words! Words! They are only vehicles to convey meanings. Words can change lives only when relationships parallel their message.

Christian persons have used words as a medium of communication but have often forgotten that living makes the message of words take on shape and content. Parents may teach youth one form of behavior but practice another; this kind of inconsistency does not encourage Christian nurture. One father in attempting to help his sons use proper language said, "Now you boys must stop your 'damn' swearing." This attempt of nurture was only words and left no positive influence.

A Sunday-school teacher may be speaking to a class of juniors and say, "Now, children, God is your loving heavenly Father." One little boy may say to himself, "If God is like my dad, I don't want anything to do with Him." *Words are empty if hearts are not full.* When the life corresponds to the message, positive change is more likely to take place.

The Word of God is different from our words. It is backed by a life. Its message stands. When the words we use to explain the Word of God are not paralleled by a consistent life, the message may become blurred and even lost.

If John sees his father reading his Bible, going to church regularly, and living daily what he reads and hears, it is more likely that he will want to do the same. However, if John knows his father uses every means to outdo his customers, and that he is concerned only about his own selfish wishes, the reading of the Bible and church attendance, even proper outward appearance, will become repulsive to him.

Persons may become formed or deformed through relationships. They can also become reformed and transformed if the persons involved are true Christians. Words only make relationships clearer.

Often the unspoken makes a more lasting impression than the use of the tongue.

Nurture is for life and by life. It is not done overnight. It is the result of encounter concerning things that matter, cemented by love, consistency, and Christian understanding. *Inconsistent living negates teaching by words.*

DECISIONS FOR LEARNING

If persons who are governed by decisions help to make those decisions, they will become more deeply involved in their purpose. Decision-making is a large part of the learning process. Youth must be allowed freedom to make decisions. It is not the task of parents to make decisions for youth, but to give them the training which will prepare them to make wise choices. Real learning takes place in decision-making. But what if youth make wrong choices? This is part of the process.

Making a youth's decision for him is a simple thing for parents. They may feel that they are saving time, and being of great assistance to the child who is so young, tender, and ill-informed. The parent is really doing the youth a grave injustice by making his decisions for him. The attitude of the youth toward his parents may undergo much negative reaction when his parents make all his decisions.

As the adolescent views the problem, the authoritarian relationships in the family do not seem to consider his need to find proper self-direction. He resents unexplained authority and requirements. Resentment is aroused when a youth is not considered as an individual with his own rights. Even though youth must make their own decisions, parents should be close enough to offer assistance and to lend encouragement and moral support when needed. [1]

The following is an example of how one youth reacted to a lack of support from the father:

I always asked how he wanted something done before I did it. Because if I didn't, I'd feel that I was doing it wrong, and he would not be satisfied with what I had done. I don't think he ever praised me for any accomplishments that I did. I won many awards in high school and also played on the main basketball team, but seldom if ever would he say anything about it. When I was around him, I did not feel like talking and sharing my problems with him because I felt he wasn't interested and I felt he probably would tell me I was too young to be thinking about such things. I wanted to know about sex and every time I would mention it to him he would tell me I was too little or too young to understand. So I just stopped asking him and found out through other means. . . . I didn't know whether he was behind my efforts or not. He has never said, but he has inferred many times that he wished I were back on the farm helping him. So I don't know how he feels about my being in school. I would like to know where he stands, but I can't bring myself to asking him or talking about it. [2]

Here is evidenced a lack of communication and support in the process of facing problems. This youth was completely on his own when he had to face decisions. He did not have the assurance of an interested parent to fall back on when needed.

In a study of Mennonite teenagers, evidence indicated that the youth showing withdrawing tendencies had had less freedom than the outgoing youth in relation to making personal decisions. It was found also that the family of the withdrawn youth engaged in less activity as a family. [3] Indecision seems to be a common theme running through the self-reports of many Mennonite youth. Fluctuation, marked by an inability to make decisions, is very common. [4]

Youth must have opportunity to make decisions under guidance. When this experience is not provided, youth may become dependent. The ability to make responsible decisions will not be present. Youth then turn to the nearest means of support at the time, and this is often undesirable assistance. If parents and pastors will not listen, youth will turn to those who will. "Dad and Mom just don't have time," is often the cry of young people.

Decision-making has a large influence on personality development. It must start in the early years of the child, and be graduated according to his understanding. Decisions need to be made first by the child in small things, such as the choice of clothing, shoes, or what clothing he is going to wear on a particular day. The choice may not always correspond with that of the parent. Here helpful guidance can be given. Decisions such as these must be increased and lead on to deeper and more meaningful decisions. Adjustment in youth and decision-making are related. [5]

Demands may be pushed upon a youth for major decisions at too early an age. This may work against personal emotional security and self-confidence. This happens especially when the decisions are not favorable.

Youth should become acquainted with such Scripture as Proverbs 3:6: "In all thy ways acknowledge him, and he shall direct thy paths." In meaningful relationships this admonition becomes reality.

Youth must be taught that decisions have consequences. The outcomes of decision-making must be faced realistically. When parents bear the consequences of decision-making for the child, the result is an experience of overdependence. As youth develop, decisions will involve increasing demands. One cannot make decisions and then run away. If Henry spends his savings on a new car and has no money for other activities, he must live with his decision. The implications of one's own choices are always before him. Some choices are of a minor description and the consequences may not involve other individuals and their welfare. To alter one's course of action on the basis of such a decision may not be very involving. Where the implications of a decision reach to the lives of other individuals, special care must be taken to maintain both self-respect and the respect of others.

An additional part of decision-making is the presence and power of the Holy Spirit in the life of the Christian. A Christian does not belong to himself. His life is always to be subject to the first claims of the Spirit. When a person can look at all angles of an issue and bring himself without bias to a neutral position, it is then that the Spirit at work within the mind of the individual can bring direction for action. The person of the Spirit has been sorely neglected in decision-making. He must be taken into account in all of life. Youth must be taught that life which is to be lived under the lordship of Jesus Christ is a trust to be controlled by the guidance of the Spirit.

If parents demonstrate a confidence in and close awareness of the Spirit's presence and power, it will be much easier for youth to make the Spirit a welcome guest in decision-making.

Youth should be helped to gather the facts, to study the implications and results of decisions, and be encouraged to move ahead with confidence.

Commitment is also a decision. Many youth find commitment too demanding. They feel a greater sense of security in a lack of commitment. When a commitment is made, action is expected. To refrain from commitment means less responsibility for meaningful action. A youth may say, "I don't care to make a decision yet, for if I do, then I must act, and I am not ready."

Youth must realize that all of life is lived in some kind of commitment. The question is not so much whether one is committed or not, but rather, to what is one committed?

Here choices are inevitable. They must be made. Several ways are usually possible. Guidance must be given so that youth may make the choice leading to commitment on the deepest level, which is commitment to Christ. That is the kind of commitment which is masterful and leads to responsible action.

It is only the deeply committed person who is the free person. Freedom comes in being committed to a cause greater than oneself. Man's real purpose for being is beyond himself. This kind of commitment calls for responsible decision-making. Decisions must be made on one's own initiative.

When decision-making is taught and opportunity is given to develop the ability to make decisions, the church will profit by individuals who are able to enter into deep commitment rather than halfhearted spiritual relationships.

TENSIONS CAN BE PRODUCTIVE

Learning results from responding to problems. The Christian Nurture Study Committee found that Mennonite youth experience a wide range of problems. They appear ready to discuss these problems and seem to be open for help. Studies suggest that problems centering on the relationship of youth to parents are most frequent. Other problem areas are relationships with youth of the same age, relationships with brothers and sisters, self-understanding, self-acceptance, acceptance of church standards, and relationships with church leaders. Beneath youth's problems is a desperate search for meaning and purpose. [6]

Some youth say, "I know one kind of home I don't want, that is, one like my parents have." They may also report, "I know the kind of home I want--one like my parents have." Wherever people are in relationships, tensions will come. Tensions can be helpful or they can cause much conflict and difficulty.

Conflict between parents and children may be caused by the attitudes of parents. Some parents are too critical, too strict, too inconsistent, or too distant to be of much help to their youth. Other parents may criticize their children so much that the children feel defeated. Some youth grow up under such a strict home pattern that later on they find it very difficult to receive direction from school, church, or anyone else, including God. This can be a result of rebellion against authority as well as a lack of proper respect for persons in authority. Some parents attempt to teach verbally but fail to be able to live a life consistent with what they say. Other parents spend so much time making money, attempting to meet the physical needs of their children, that they never really get close enough to know them. [7]

Tensions can develop on many levels. Tensions may result from negative reaction to strict control. It appears that resentment is often directed toward misunderstood authority and demands. Resentment is also aroused when youth are not considered as individuals.

A second point of tension may be poor parent-youth communication. Communication is a universal problem. In relation to the family, many youth feel that their ideas are not considered nor given audience. Parents do not share information with their youth which they badly need. They are not sufficiently concerned about the youth's needs. Youth feel pressure from this lack of communication in two ways. They feel that they are not able to make a meaningful contribution to life, and that they are of little value.

A third point of tension seems to be found in the amount of affection shown to youth. Some youth feel a lack of affection from both their parents and their brothers and sisters. They may even wonder whether they are being loved and accepted at all. Some youth are concerned about the lack of the expression of love between their parents or between their brothers and sisters. This lack of affection causes some to wonder whether they have any use in the world. Because of the lack of love expressed at home some youth have contemplated suicide, and some running away from home to see if they are missed. Some youth feel that they must meet a certain level of performance, either exceptionally high or exceptionally low, to be accepted. They know this is not healthy, but it is one way to get attention.

A fourth tension point is found in the level of family standards which may often pose a handicap to acceptance in the community, especially if they are exceptionally low. A number of youth feel ashamed of their family when it is compared with others in the community.'

Youth are growing in social consciousness and if their home does not compare favorably with others, tensions and dissatisfaction may result. Good family relationships can make up for a lack of physical surroundings. The atmosphere is far more important than the gadgets that are provided for youth.

A fifth point of tension is that of dependency upon youth's friends. Such dependency patterns, especially the overindulgent ones, may stem from feelings of insecurity at home. At times these relationships can become so strong that if broken, they can create much difficulty. Strained parental relationships often drive youth to the establishment of relationships, which they so badly need, in some other context. [8]

Among other tension points that might be mentioned is the parental desire for the social progress of the child. Perhaps the parents were unable to attain a certain level of living, and fulfillment of personal ambitions; as a result they may find themselves either consciously or unconsciously thrusting their child into situations where he may be a complete misfit. Some religious people may find it undesirable to enter certain vocations, and so consequently force their children to seek approval through certain positions in the religious group. Where a person is expected to reach a certain level but finds himself unable, tension results which may create much unhappiness and internal frustration. [9]

There is, without a doubt, considerable variation in the capacity for frustration among youth. A proportion of mental illness found in adults may be the result of delayed frustrations and tensions during youth. [10]

Adolescent adjustment often reflects the personality of the parents. One study showed that mothers of emotionally disturbed adolescent girls were distinguished from mothers of normal girls of the same age in several ways. The mothers of the emotionally disturbed girls imposed their plans upon their daughters, they were overpossessive, they were not frank with their daughters, their relations with the father were strained, and they were overanxious. [11]

Problems of development often stem from personality faults in the parents. Adolescents are quick to note such faults. There is no substitute for being a real person. What adults say is not as important as what they do and what they are. [12]

Feelings of frustration produce hostility. Hostility is a very disturbing emotion. It can lead to destructive consequences. Both the home and the church should attempt to understand the causes of hostility and cope with them with great care. Hostility can be a symptom of distress ranging from mild irritation to acute anguish. It may show itself in different forms, such as anger, rage, or resentment. [13]

Hostile behavior is somewhat like an armor. It can be a kind of defense behind which personal wishes can operate. Hostility can be spoken of as a kind of defense or cover-up. [14]

Tension must be faced and dealt with objectively. Not all tensions are undesirable. Some tensions can be very helpful. If there is tension between the youth and Christ, he needs to be helped to understand, and submit to Christ's lordship. Christ is able to give great help in overcoming unwholesome tensions. It is desirable to have the point of tension between youth and unchristian belief and action. This kind of tension is profitable and must be understood and guided.

A study of senior students in eight Christian high schools [15] revealed the following areas in the experience of youth that point up both wholesome and unwholesome points of tension.

Insincerity and hypocrisy seem to be pet peeves. Fear of war is prominent among youth. Emotional sensitivity is extreme, especially among the girls. A large percentage feel like crying. This may call for a number interpretations. There seems to be fair social integration, since most youth generally participate in group activities and do not usually feel excluded. Many Mennonite youth feel that they have good times at home and are proud of their parents. Many of them feel wanted at home and sense their parents' love through their actions. Mennonite youth tend to take a stronger stand against drinking and smoking than against cheating in school. A surprisingly large group dance, or would dance if they had the opportunity. This is strange for a group that traditionally has taken a strong stand against the dance in any form. A kiss seems no longer to be a seal for betrothal, as it was once considered to be. Many Mennonite youth would like to be free to date and marry non-Mennonites, rather than be restricted to their own group. Necking and petting are fairly popular pastimes among youth. A serious factor here is the percentage of youth who feel there is harm in it but engage in it nevertheless. Youth get less sex information from parents than from any other source. Worship is high on the list as motivation for church attendance. Christian assurance and emphasis on attire are live religious issues. Most religious experiences are initiated between the ages of ten and thirteen. A majority of youth believe in the efficacy of prayer. Youth in general seem to have a desire for more contacts by pastors and church leaders.

The Christian high-school senior presents a rather composite picture of Mennonite youth. He is inclined to reflect the characteristics of his age level. He does not appear to do too much thinking for himself. He respects his parents but needs more skillfully given counsel. There is a tendency to stress overt matters and ignore those that reflect real inner moral integrity. In dating experiences, even though he may question the rightness of certain practices, he tends to conform to the norm. The answers he gets for his problems are spiritually familiar answers. There is a sense of uncertainty and bewilderment present in his life. Perhaps the high regard Mennonite youth have for the Scriptures, if they can be made practical, points the way to help for the majority of youth.

Where religion is a dominant factor in the life of a people, there is much more cause for tension. Religion can be restrictive. Youth want something to live for, not just things to refrain from.

Tensions must be faced and understood for what they are. They must be dealt with fairly. It will never be possible to alleviate all tension. This would not be good even if it were possible. Wholesome tensions must be utilized, and unwholesome tensions must be understood and alleviated by careful planning and guidance.

THINGS THAT MATTER

The more secure a youth is emotionally, the more likely it is that he will possess a greater degree of spiritual maturity. Youth have a deep need to feel loved, needed, and understood while moving to adulthood. In this process, some growing pains can be expected. Youth have a deep need to reach beyond themselves, to associate meaningfully with others, and to commit themselves to a cause. They seek to meet their spiritual, psychological, and physical needs as they see them. Failure to meet these needs can lead to frustration and tension. Frustrations and stress can serve a useful purpose, but they become harmful when they are too great to handle, or when they arise out of misunderstanding of the self, or through exploitation of others. [16]

Mennonite youth have problems that are unique to them as members of a small religious group. These problems may cause frustration or may be the means of providing unique learning experiences.

The doctrine of nonresistance is a major belief of the Mennonite Church. From its beginning this religious group has always adhered to the doctrine of the way of love. This involves the return of loving action for acts of hatred. As a theology there should be little difficulty following such a doctrine; however, in practice some problems appear. Studies of human nature are increasingly pointing out that one cannot repress hostility continually if mental health is to be retained. It is difficult for a person, especially a youth, to react in a loving fashion if he is continually the recipient of hostility. Youth can react in one of two ways. They may repress their hostilities, which will later complicate the situation, or they may respond by exercising behavior which acts out their frustration.

Another result of the doctrine of nonresistance might be the rejection of the Mennonite way of life when inconsistency is noted between the belief and the actual practice. Youth are idealistic and have little tolerance for differences between the ideal and the real.

The difference between the ideal and the real is easily seen by youth. This should challenge parents and church leaders to a pattern of action that is consistent.

There are areas beyond nonresistance where problems emerge. For example, the doctrine of world mission and the universal need for the Gospel. If youth see only the results of conformity in the local congregation and a lack of creativity and mission, the doctrine simply seems to be word magic. Youth begin to question whether the church really believes what it says or whether it believes one thing and practices on an entirely different level.

The doctrine of adult membership is an additional area which creates conflict for the adolescent. Traditionally, Mennonites have held to adult membership. Youth, while becoming members, are not considered in every way bona fide members. A youth because of his lack of maturity and experience is often not considered on the same level as an adult member. He is, however, expected to take on the manner of life of the adult member. The adolescent is caught in a situation in which he theoretically should not be a member, but in actuality is hemmed in and encouraged in many ways to become one. This period of induction into the responsibilities of full membership can create difficulty if the expectations are higher than the ability to perform.

The adolescent is also subject to an additional problem. This is one of knowing where to identify. Subjection to the group has been a basic issue in the Mennonite way of life. In the larger culture the free-floating individual is often held up as the ideal. The identities of the Mennonite group and the larger culture are in conflict. Youth want to become loyal sons of the Mennonite Church but may be restricted in self-development, as they see it from the angle of the larger culture. Because the Mennonite Church is in transition from an isolated sect to a more urban type of religious group, many youth are left with an unclear picture in relation to what self-image they should develop. [17]

Youth have two basic needs. One is the need to develop a sense of personhood and self-identity. The second is the need to relate meaningfully to others. The process through which these needs can be fulfilled is through proper understanding of self and others. Personhood, self-identity, and awareness come largely through relationships with those persons who seem significant to youth. In this process the early years are very important. As a youth grows in his awareness of God's love and the love of those around him, he develops an awareness of his personal need to reach out to others and give himself in meaningful relationships.

Problems may arise when these needs in youth are not adequately met. A loss of a sense of personal identity or a lack of acceptance may lead to a deep feeling of insecurity and frustration. These in turn may be expressed through withdrawal, conformity, or through patterns of hostility and aggression. Such feelings may be directed toward oneself, others, the community, or the church. The person may surrender his personal identity to the group in his search for acceptance unless he has been able to develop a meaningful understanding of self. It is possible that he may move into an extreme individualism if he has become afraid of trusting himself in a meaningful relationship to others. Health of mind depends upon the degree to which these basic needs become met.

Some students of human development agree that frustration is a necessary factor in movement toward maturity. Frustration leads to a search for helpful solutions to personal problems. It is harmful when it becomes greater than the individual can bear or when it is related to irrational fears. [18] Youth react to a problem in one of three ways. They may avoid it, defy it, or cope with it. [19] In fact, all life situations can be dealt with in one of these ways.

Youth must be taught to cope with problems rather than follow the other two alternatives. Take hostility for example. It must be faced and understood. What can a Christian do about hostility? It should be recognized as felt, and not suppressed. One must accept his feelings in order to be able to work with them. A second step in dealing with hostility is to look within and discover the contributing cause of the feelings. A person may find attitudes and actions that need to be understood and adjusted. Feelings of hostility growing out of childhood may be transferred to present situations. A third step in dealing with hostility is to try to build better relationships with the person toward whom one has wrong feelings. [20] The Bible teaches that one should go directly to the person who has anything against him and work for reconciliation. [21]

One's living creates needs. There are five basic needs that youth have due to their humanity. They need to be related, to rise beyond themselves, to be rooted, to be known, and to feel at home. [22] Most all problems that emerge may stem from any one of these basic needs. They may also provide helpful learning situations.

To be related is a basic need. Relatedness must be developed with others and with God. If there are proper relationships at home, relation to God takes on deeper meaning. Likewise, the master commitment to Jesus Christ assists greatly in one's relationships to others. Youth are social beings and find meaning in relationships. When this experience is not what it could or should be, a deep sense of need is created. Lack of effectiveness in this area in the life of youth may bring deep discouragement and a sense of failure. Understanding counsel and guidance must be exercised in helping youth who have experienced these.

The ability to rise beyond oneself is the second need. One can become so discouraged by his humanity that he is never able to rise. On the other hand, it is possible for a youth to become so removed from himself and related to the idealistic that he cannot objectively look at his own deep needs. There is a healthy middle position where a youth can look at himself, through the Word, by listening to the Spirit and to one's fellowmen. He is then able to rise beyond his own self through the power of God.

The third need of youth is rootedness. They need a sense of security and of belongingness. This can be developed in the home. When a youth develops an awareness of being needed, that he matters to someone, that someone cares, rootedness takes place. It is possible for one to become too stationary, and make little progress. The kind of rootedness that is most helpful is rootedness that relates a youth to Christ and to his fellowmen in meaningful relationships.

The fourth need of youth is to be known and to know. A youth must be able to identify himself in God's universe. Identity is essential to finding meaning in life. A youth develops no meaningful sense of identity if he has no frame of reference from which to relate meaningfully to others. A youth must learn to know himself, God, and others in the world in which he has been placed.

Youth's fifth need is that of feeling at home. A sense of at-homeness and at-oneness is important. A frame of reference out of which to live and serve is essential to meaning and happiness. This comes through developing Christian relationships in the home, the church, and the community. Proper relationships with man are essential for proper relatedness to God. The same can be said in reverse.

Youth who have a secure home background, who have good interpersonal relationships, are usually better prepared than others to face life. All life's experiences must be taken as God's will for a Christian. If experiences arise out of one's sheer foolishness or unwise activity, God cannot be held accountable. Even in cases such as this, if youth can fall back on parents or friends who understand and care, it will be likely that they will come through with a greater degree of purposefulness.

Life is a classroom. All experiences should be made meaningful by parents and other leaders who care.

TEACHING FOR LIVING

To be committed to a cause greater than oneself is real living, when this cause is bound to Jesus Christ.

Christianity seeks to conform all human reason and its achievements to Jesus Christ, Creator, Redeemer, and Judge. For this reason it has a deep abiding interest in education and culture. It summons all personal and social life to the lordship of Jesus Christ. [2 3]

The problem of selecting, preparing for, and entering a vocation faces most youth. Behind this pursuit lies the basic question of discovering the meaning of vocation in a Christian sense. The degree of choice may be limited. Economic factors, culture, and scientific progress all have their influence upon vocational choice. The work a person does should provide at least a measure of satisfaction. This may provide a starting basis for choosing a vocation. In addition the problem of economic support is no small item in the highly industrialized age in which youth find themselves. The problem of find-ing an opening in the field in which one is gifted and prepared is a constant threat. The rapidly changing occupational pattern, in Western culture in particular, is another complex problem all youth face. [24]

Many youth are leaving the vocation of farming which was once considered to be the one occupational mold which provided the type of context into which Mennonites and the Mennonite way of life could be cast. This picture has changed much in recent years and will continue to make great changes. The trend in urbanization has also painted a different picture for Mennonite occupational choices.

How do youth choose a vocation? Is it purely on the basis of work available? Do aptitude and preference have any influence? Should parental planning enter the picture? Last, but not least, where does the lordship of Christ fit into the total vocational scheme?

Certainly one's abilities should be discovered and trained so that one's potential might be realized. Most youth should have at least one year of training beyond secondary education. This may help greatly in determining the type of work for which they are fitted. At this point decision can be made concerning the vocational direction to be taken.

Parents should assist a youth in discovering his native ability. They should assist in his training and preparation, not forcing him into a prescribed mold, or urging him to fulfill some latent vocational desire of their own.

Certainly youth should make vocational choice a special matter of prayer and seek carefully the location and the type of occupation through which the Lord would have them invest their talents.

Careful counseling with both parents and pastor is very important in finding the place and the type of occupation into which a youth should thrust himself.

While there are many side benefits from a vocation, the basic factor is the contribution one is able to make for Christ and the church. It is not the church's task, basically, to build the kingdom, but to inherit it and assist others in doing the same. God is using individuals in making known the conditions of inheritance.

The basic concern is not finding the right vocation but being the right kind of person in the vocation where one finds himself. This is not to preclude careful choice for special kinds of contributions that need to be made. It is simply saying that a Christian witness is needed in and through all vocations that do not militate against Christian ethics.

Serious and effective Christian witness is the result of being the right kind of person. It is possible to make youth too vocation-conscious. Levels of service can be labeled to the degree that some will strongly feel that they are serving the Lord, while others in a lesser occupation are only laboring for a living. Christ must be central in all vocations.

Personal abilities and desires must be taken into consideration along with the needs that exist. The basic objective in service must always be kept clearly in view. Serving is both for the welfare of one's fellow brother and for the development of the individual involved. When service becomes an end in itself, and all become servants of an organization or structure, service has missed its basic thrust.

A part of doing is for the purpose of becoming. The basic motivation should come from the love action of God made plain through the Word of the Gospel. Service should never exist for personal merit alone, but in response to existing need and opportunity.

The Christian Church does not have a mission; it is basically mission. Its task is to make known the claims of the lordship of Jesus Christ. It must use vocation for paying the expenses and as an avenue for fulfilling mission. The church that isolates the two is missing its basic calling. To be the church in the community where it is found is the primary responsibility of every congregation. Reaching beyond its borders can be compensation for failing to meet the needs at its own doorstep. There must be personal encounter for church and community betterment. Commitment and involvement through unselfish living must be the rule of the day in every community where Christ would be known.

Bridges of understanding must be built rather than barriers of isolation constructed. Christianity must never become a wall but must increasingly bridge the gap for world understanding. The community and God must be brought to terms with each other. The church is the agent and the individual the personality God would use to perform this reconciliation. Youth must be prepared for this task.

When the history of this generation is written, the noticable thing will be, not so much the noise of the wicked, but the appalling silence of the good. [25] Christians must relate to need to be of any help.

We may have great respect for those reformers who started movements which assisted in the removal of great social evils, but we have little time to commend those who stand out from the crowd to point out our own evils. Children of some revolutionaries of past days are proud of their ancestors, but these same children go to great length to curb revolutionary ideas in their own offspring. [26]

Youth should be given freedom of choice. They should be provided with inner equipment to be able to make right choices, and to follow through with meaningful action.

Youth who take an active part in church life and work are usually better prepared to assist in meeting the needs of their fellowmen than are those who do not become deeply involved in church life and work. [27]

The church has many youth entering service programs who are making a meaningful contribution. These youth usually come from homes where a spiritual atmosphere prevailed and where the lordship of Jesus Christ was given a prominent place. [28]

The day is upon us when the church should give its homes greater assistance in building persons for mission. The church will need to lay hands upon its talented youth as rapidly as they can be secured. The church needs everyone if she is only able to sense it. [29] The personal conviction of youth should not be exploited, but should be trusted to responsible individuals.

Nurture should be kept in focus. The basic thrust of Christian nurture is the new self in Christ, mature and responsible, with a grasp upon the true meaning of life. Christian nurture deals with the process of being and becoming. Preparation should be a result of call and conviction as over against desire for prestige and financial accumulation. Service should be considered a privilege and not a duty.

Youth can develop purpose for living. Individuals with little purpose make little contribution. A sense of worth, dignity, and fulfillment needs to be developed so that life may be faced with meaning.

Service is a result of a love relationship. It should be motivated by a love greater than that of personal benefit. Freedom should be found through commitment. A person gains freedom, not by rebellion or unplanned living, but by making responsible choices. [30]

Responsible choice-making comes as a result of Christian nurture. Maturity is the end of nurture, maturity in Jesus Christ and the fellowship of believers.

Youth are a heritage. They are priceless. The responsibility they afford is always before the home and the church. Every effort will need to be put forth both to understand and to be understood, both to teach and to learn. Parents and all youth leaders should make themselves available, through sincere dedication and consistency of life and action, for Christian nurture.

Nurture is a lifelong responsibility. Its meaning will need to be understood more clearly by youth, parents, and church leaders for effective results. *Every life situation, if properly used, can become one of life's best classrooms. Real learning is experienced in the context of living relationships. The development of youth can be planned. Planning the actual experiences of life may not be as important as planning the right environment where experiences can happen.*

2 YOUTH NEED A MODEL

Christ can change lives best as those in need of change see Him at work in the lives of others. How is youth to relate to Christ? How does Christ cause change in the life of youth? Is the Christian life relevant for youth or is it basically for older individuals who have reached a degree of maturity which makes Christian living easier? If Christianity is for youth, how does one measure progress, and how can one be sure that a particular youth is measuring up to a desirable level of maturity? Does Christ really make a difference in a person's life, or is the change merely psychological in origin, and the pattern of Christ only one more for imitation? Questions such as these are real. There are no easy answers.

Augustine asked, If man was not made for God, why is he so unhappy apart from God? Man was created in God's image for His glory. Man is unhappy apart from a proper relationship to God. Man must relate to God to find meaning in life. This can and does begin in youth. High spiritual expectations are not out of order for youth. There need not be a period of lavish sinning or sowing of wild oats before one comes to the Lord for mercy and pardon. Persons are basically sinful and it does not take too many encounters with the evil one for this awareness to become reality. We are sinful beings in need of the mercy of God from youth. Beginning at the age of accountability this awareness strikes one full force. When youth recognize their sinful nature as over against their sins, a sense of accountability is developing.

The new birth is a clear spiritual demand in Scripture[1] for admission into the kingdom of God. A new creation[2] is the result of the power of God at work in the heart of man. Conversion is a right-about-face, a turning in the opposite direction. It is a readying of oneself for the power of God to perform the operation that all need, the changed heart. The new birth which comes as a result of the union of the faith of man and the grace of God results in a movement from self-centeredness to Christ-centeredness. This movement is begun and completed by the Holy Spirit. Regeneration may actually have implications that are not all realized at the time. While some of the aspects of regeneration are in the realm of conscious awareness, some may be in the realm of the subconscious and only become reality in the life of youth at the point of meaningful experience with reality. This means that the presence of Christ and His power is then a constant necessity for giving guidance in the life of the newborn spiritual child so that he can successfully face the new encounters of daily living.

Temptation comes to all. It is not sinful; it must be faced and overcome. Growth may be measured by the level of one's temptations. If a person is tripping over the same logs at fifty as at eighteen, perhaps he has not grown. *Maybe one should have a new set of temptations periodically?*

This is one reason why being born again is not sufficient in itself. One must appropriate the presence of Christ and His Spirit daily for the reshaping of one's self into a more perfect image of the Creator.

The Covenant Theory of the Reformed tradition teaches that all children born to Christian parents and reared in a Christian family are children of God. In Anabaptist belief children are, at the age of accountability, responsible persons under God, and must exercise their powers of choice. The environment of a Christian home is not to be minimized at all. It should lay the framework in which a responsible decision will be made more easily and intelligently. Children before accountability are "safe" and should perhaps not be classed as saved until regeneration takes place. They are safe because of the atonement and its implications for individuals who are not able to make responsible choices. An innocent youth should not be hastened to the confessional. He should rather be reared in an atmosphere of love and acceptance so that when the conscious awareness of his sinnerhood settles upon him, he may make an intelligent decision for Christ, who provided salvation for everyone.

The overemphasis of depravity in childhood leads to premature decisions, and militates against a more mature experience by youth in relation to the lordship of Jesus Christ. Christianity is a way of life. It is to be chosen responsibly. It is for both youth and adult life. Its demands are far-reaching. It must be encountered, weighed, and decisively entered. It is possible that some may not be able to lay their finger upon the time and place of their conversion. They seem to have known nothing other than being a Christian. Some persons being raised in a meaningful Christian environment, and who were exceptionally responsive to the claims of Christ, might not remember a crisis experience of turning from darkness to light. This might be classed as a slow and unpainful birth, a gradual growing into the image and likeness of Christ. This is, however, not without a responsible choice for this way of life, whether instantaneous or prolonged.

The environment of both home and church aids much in setting the pattern of conversion. Parents are the logical persons to lead youth to meaningful relationship with Christ. *Where parents are authoritarian and inconsistent, conversion age tends to be either premature or prolonged.* A high degree of authority also lessens the probability that a youth will seek help from either parent or pastor in the conversion experience. The help of an evangelist or of other persons not as directly associated with the youth is often sought.

After a youth is led to Christ, his life must still be fashioned. It must and will be formed. A careful pattern must be planned by pastors and parents.

WHO IS MATURE?

Youth need a model. If they do not find this model in Christ exemplified through parents, pastors, and friends, they invariably turn to other sources. Christ is able to provide for youth the pattern that is needed. *Christ is not yellow or red, but dynamic, relevant, alive, and present.* He is able to speak youth's language, understand their tensions, meet their inner longings, and shape their lives. Christ provides a true basis for being a person. He offers grace instead of achievement. It is then possible to maintain a sense of worth despite one's failures and sins. Christ is also an ideal with which one may identify in order to deal with failure and sin. He is a model worthy of aspiration. In addition, Christ provides a model for relating to other persons. He demonstrates acceptance and love for all persons. Christ gives true meaning and purpose to life. Loyalty to Christ develops Christian personality and provides a basis for making meaningful decisions. [3]

The New Testament recognized that one's behavior may fall short of his intentions. All Christians fall short of the perfect will of God. It is through the grace of God revealed in Jesus Christ that youth can experience acceptance in spite of shortcomings. Youth who are aware of temptations, who experience anger, jealousy, carnality, rebellion, and pride, need not give up, or despair, even when yielding to temptation momentarily. Christ is able to bring them through if they are able to develop the proper faith relationship.

What Christ does for the believer He does through the Holy Spirit. The Holy Spirit has truly been called the "executive secretary of the Godhead." He is present to help youth in a number of ways.

In the first place, it is the Spirit of God who unites the convert to Christ and makes meaningful His relation to the Christian. The Spirit uses the Word of God in the context of the Christian fellowship to bring assurance to the heart of the believer.

Secondly, the Spirit of Christ creates a hunger or a holy desire for Christian growth. Becoming a Christian is not merely a decision of prudence; it is a response to the wooing power of the Holy Spirit. God must convict and work in the heart of an individual or he will not be converted. The born-again disciple is then eager to know the will of God and grow in the Christian graces. He will have an increasing desire to know and do the will of God more perfectly.

In the third place, it is not enough for the Spirit to assist the person in seeing his need of growth, but He also must provide divine enablement to live and serve as Christ did. [4] The Christian experience is not something to imitate by drawing upon one's personal resources. It is a matter of walking in the Spirit in each human relationship. The Spirit puts to death the works of the flesh and enables victory over, and sets one free from, the bondage of sin and sinful habits. It is the Spirit who grants strength for holy living. It must be understood, however, that all Christians stand in need of the grace of God and forgiveness as long as they live. Christ employs nurture for maturity both before and after conversion. Faith, vocation, doctrines and practices, and courtship are a few of the problem areas in and through which youth need careful guidance from understanding parents and pastors. [5]

A sound conversion does not mean that youth have no need of ethical instruction. A person may experience a sound conversion and may be ignorant of the ethics of the Christian way of life. A close affinity to the Word and meaningful exchange in fellowship with God's people will assist in the formulation of clear ethical conviction and practice. *A teaching program that sells rather than forces is of crucial importance in the nurture of youth.*

There are no shortcuts to Christian maturity. It is a lifelong process. Bible reading, prayer, fellowship, obedience, stewardship, regular participation in the life of the gathered as well as the scattered church are ingredients which lead to a more mature life. Maturity is stimulated by Christ and the Spirit and guided by the Word and Christian fellowship.

Unfortunately both parents and church leaders may condition youth toward a negative attitude in relation to Christianity. Inconsistency, harshness, lack of love and acceptance by those posing as Christians may encourage some youth to make up their minds never to become Christians. A home and church in which there is love, happiness, a sense of purpose, unselfishness, sincere, quiet leadership, yet firm and objective, will exert much influence toward the youth's happy acceptance of Christ and the Christian way of life. *Christian environment will provide opportunity for a happy preconversion experience in the life of children and will lead them eventually to a meaningful commitment in adolescence.*

WHAT TO EXPECT

Paul established goals for his life. He set a standard of attainment, and expected other Christians to be as concerned about spiritual growth and improvement as he was. In Philippians[6] Paul allows a little insight into his marathon race. He says, "I press toward the mark." Who had established his goal? How did he set a level of expectancy for himself? Did his relation to others or his position as a spiritual leader have anything to do with his goals? *Does responsibility encourage more responsible behavior?* Are we to set a standard for youth, as adults, and then stand off and watch them try and fail? What is the ideal Christian youth like? Toward what are we aiming?

To set a norm for behavior is difficult. One can only, on the basis of Scripture, sound judgment, and careful counsel, come near to what a pattern for life and behavior should include for maturing youth. Some guiding principles might be the following. In the care of their bodies Christian youth should maintain good health through proper rest and exercise; refraining from the use of tobacco, alcoholic drinks, or dangerous drugs. Some will, because of their convictions and goals, enter college. Vocational preparation and education should be held in esteem. Youth should have sincerely sought and turned to Christ in repentance and faith, experienced a meaningful baptism, and should be enjoying growth as Christians. They will develop a wholesome self-image, and view themselves as youth of sound character. They will live a clean moral life, choosing a life characterized by continence until marriage. They will develop an interest in the opposite sex, and also maintain meaningful friendships with those of their own sex. They will read the Bible with a high degree of regularity and will spend time in prayer. Their growing Christian life will be characterized by regular church attendance and Christian fellowship. They will grow to love the church of their choice and sense acceptance in its program. They will develop a sense of appreciation for their denomination and a concern for its welfare and growth. They will want to be intelligent Christians concerned about both what and why they believe. They will have a growing ability to give a clear account of their faith and its practical daily implications. They will have a strong sense of becoming independent personalities but will love and respect authority.

They will work through their brother-sister tensions. They will be concerned for the welfare of each family member. They will have a growing desire to make a contribution "in the name of Christ" to society. They will have respect for both their culture and their government. They will desire to find their place in society for the purpose of constructive behavior. They will think of their health and strength and their financial resources as gifts from God to be used responsibly. They will seek to find the vocation that would bring both personal satisfaction, glory to God, and assistance to their fellowmen. They will consider Christian vocation in and through the church as a first and meaningful challenge. They will enhance the name "Christian" by high ideals, by endeavor to serve, and by the reality of their faith. While youth may not consistently attain these goals, their desire to grow along with a sincere effort to find perfection in Christ will characterize their lives. [7]

Sometimes adult standards are imposed upon youth at too early an age. The frustrations held by both parents and church leaders, because of their inability to maintain a certain level in their own experience, can be the basis of too high demands and expectations. Standards set at a higher level than youth are able to attain produce tensions and conflicts that invariably cause undesirable results.

Goals need to be understood. Standards provide a pattern, a level toward which to move. Goals should be set high enough to provide a challenge, but not so high as to be beyond the possibilities of achievement. Objectives for youth should be consistent, Biblical in origin, and relevant to youth's particular life problems.

A well-adjusted youth is one who is able to "accommodate" to the aspects of his environment that are relatively fixed and unchanging, and at the same time develop the ability to "interact" with those aspects of his environment which are changeable, especially those with sub-Christian practices. [8] This means that youth need to have a solid faith, but yet be flexible enough to see through new issues, and firm enough to resist evil.

Changes cause tension even in youth. One youth, because of strict parental control and a desire on her part to make some changes in attire, turned against Christ and the church. Which is better, being away from Christ and the church, or a few modest changes? The answer is clear. But some parents have blurred vision.

It is easy for adults, both parents and church leaders, to set standards of belief and action that are to be maintained by all family members or all church groups regardless of age. It may be possible that standards set for adult direction are frustrating to youth because of their inability to achieve certain expectations. Perhaps standards for family and church life should be graded. This would not be for the purpose of lowering behavior patterns but for the purpose of achieving a higher degree of correlation between requirements and actual behavior. It is one thing to have rule books that clearly outline a pattern of perfection for all. It is quite another to have the hearts and lives of individuals caught up in that which they believe, participating for the glory of God, even though the actual behavior pattern may be below the desirable.

It may also be possible that, for both youth and adults, participation in the drawing up of objectives, standards, or goals might be both meaningful momentarily, and stimulate a higher level of actual behavior. It is a basic principle in group work that if standards are to convey meaning to the group as a whole, they must participate in their construction. The constant fear is that laymen will draw up a set of lower standards than desirable, while the results are often standards that are more rigid than those of the pastor. It has been found that students often produce more rigid requirements when drawing up standards than do the teachers.

A risk may be involved in this kind of cooperative sharing; however, the assets far outweigh the liabilities. *Every home and congregation ought to have the experience of prayerfully and carefully working through a pattern of conduct for their members.* This pattern should be graded to take into account the understanding of various age levels. Youth want their leaders to blaze a trail in right living, but they also want to participate through discussion in the choice of that trail, especially for themselves. [9]

Desirable spiritual aims might be classed as meaningfulness, direction, the balance of authority and freedom, and maturity in love. [10] Paul's great love hymn encourages putting away the childish and becoming a man. Being tossed about by every wind of doctrine is not to be the characteristic of a mature Christian. The religion of true, mature love represents life's highest level. This is a religion of grace and acceptance rather than earned merit. It is a religion characterized by inner perception. Nourishment by the force of love is better than verbal pronouncements and affirmations.

Maturity is characterized by self-government and self-dependence as well as a balance between one's own nature and the demands of other people. The process of growth takes time to achieve fruition.[11]

The youth who was able to face a crisis and make sound decisions, it was found, had the psychological support of parents who cared. Even though they were not with him at the time, he was able to depend upon them, because he knew what kind of decision they would have made in a similar situation.

A lack of understanding of physical and mental maturation in the life of an individual may cause a parent to expect too much or too little from children.[12]

The spiritual health of Mennonite youth is favorable in comparison with other youth; however, they still have room for growth. They are not exempt from the problems that face non-Christian or other Christian youth. The kind of problems may be the same, but the degree of involvement may be less. A small proportion of Mennonite youth are exceptionally strong in faith and life, and a small proportion are overtly rejecting the Christian faith and rebelling against both home and church discipline. A considerable number are not strong in faith, witness, and service, nor are they especially defiant or negative. This middle-of-the-road apathy can be a result of a lack of involvement. *To be conformed but not involved is as serious as no relationship at all.*

As a youth matures, he should become increasingly aware of moral responsibility. Children should be allowed to make mistakes without undue excitement or the evoking of reference to serious moral consequences. A child should be encouraged to do things because of the satisfaction he receives rather than worrying about such virtues as responsibility or regularity.

There must be an increasing awareness of the moral implications of behavior. There should be a continual refining process, stimulated by a consistent pattern of behavior from both parents and other leaders. Mistakes will emerge. However, when error is in evidence, the wrong behavior has already transpired. No doubt the youth is more concerned than he appears to be. *He must be accepted and loved in spite of his behavior rather than for it.*

Trial and error are normal for all persons in most of life's experiences. In many cases trial and error are normal and helpful. There are some experiences in life, however, where trial which is known to lead to error and sin must be avoided. This implies that parents, teachers, and church leaders must carefully explain the restricted areas of life to youth, not in an attitude of legislation, but through careful discussion and sharing concerning the moral consequence and the evident results. For example, one does not need to experience fornication to learn that it is sinful.

In attempting to change attitudes, values, or behavior, the more related they are to the reason for the existence of the group, the greater will be the influence the group can exert upon the areas in which change is desired. It is also understood that the greater the attraction the group holds for the individual, the more influence it will be able to exert in the life of the individual.[13] This means that the home and church respectively should speak to the issues that are relevant to the life of youth. It also means that the persons involved in doing the speaking will need to have developed ability to listen to youth. If youth cannot see consistency and experience communication and sympathetic understanding, loyalty will not be built. *Every effort must be bent toward understanding communication and fellowship if youth are to grow up unto Him in all things.*

BUILDING IN CONTROLS

The area of self-discipline is a problem area for youth. It is apparent that many youth have never been allowed to think for themselves. They have never had opportunity to discuss their ideas with other persons or to refine their own thinking. They have apparently never been allowed to work through a program for themselves. If they are not allowed to make decisions while at home, they find it very difficult to make decisions when away from home without parental assistance. This new situation can be very frustrating because decisions need to be made. This kind of experience may lead a youth to stress and strain because of the inability to come to appropriate decisions or because of making hasty decisions, without considering the consequences. One youth found it difficult to make decisions later on in life because he was forced to make major decisions too early in life. Decision-making must be geared to the level of youth's maturity.

Due to the lack of a developing inner discipline youth find it difficult to accept responsibility. This difficulty in taking responsibility also reflects itself in group living experiences. Youth may become self-satisfied and self-centered. This kind of youth, away from home control, begins moving out in undesirable ways because the forced suppression known at home is removed.

The situation in the home which creates rebellion is often one of strict supervision, making no allowance for the development of inner discipline and controls. [14] *Youth must be given opportunity to make personal decisions.*

Controls are important. They may begin by supervising the outside environment of the life of an individual, but unless there is a process of integration by which the standard moves within the life of the person, unwholesome results will sooner or later appear.

This means youth must make some free choices. This can be overdrawn, of course; however, without freedom, responsibility cannot develop. Freedom to choose develops a sense of responsibility. Not all children are alike. One may respond more freely than another. Some may use freedom wisely at an early age and thereby merit more freedom. Each person must be understood and a pattern of operation planned for him. Freedom is given as a gift and yet it is earned. It must be appropriated to the degree that a person is able to function objectively in its presence.

In the process of developing responsibility, we should go as far as youth are ready to go. The kind of discipline we want will need to be directly related to the specific goals in mind. *To help youth acquire inner discipline requires a detailed and an intimate understanding of personality.* The method used in supporting youth in decision-making should be that of flexible watchfulness with continual reevaluation of how much the youth can take without undue frustration. [15] It is extremely important that we be able to choose the moment of receptivity in developing inner discipline. Where parents are overanxious in relation to the degree of control given youth, they must be careful that their anxiety does not become contagious and lead to a weakening rather than a supporting influence. An awareness of the changing and fluctuating needs of youth is important for the development of healthy personalities.

Inner control is no accident. It is planned, guided, integrated, but not without sacrifice. Its development is a must for healthy, wholesome living. Without it, a person becomes a dependent being with little ability to act responsibly under God and within society.

The final goal of all effort in the home, school, and community is to develop healthy Christian personalities. The achievement of inner spiritual balance is a prerequisite to feeling in tune with one's self. [16]

There are some, of course, who may feel that independence is incompatible with Christianity. We must help youth know how to be both independent and dependent at the same time. Whether it is more religious to exercise dependency rather than independency is a question that is difficult to answer. [17] One must develop a healthy balance of both for solid living. One must learn to depend upon God while developing adequate self-confidence.

People of the Middle Ages were basically tradition-directed. The American pioneers broke with much of the tradition and became inner-directed. Most Americans of today in middle-class urban society are other-directed. This implies that dependency may not be sufficient in the development of a system of control. Inner direction must be developed.

Not all religious people are of the same type, and no one person functions consistently in the same pattern. Religious persons may be open to the traditions of church fathers, but at the same time remain open to the opinion of their associates and be guided also by inner experience.

A well-balanced combination is healthful. This is why the question, "Is an independent person less religious than a dependent person?" has no immediate answer. It must be determined wherein lies the basis of both his independence and his dependence. [18] *If independence means rebellion against God, His Word, the work of the Spirit, and all things right and good, it is then destructive. If it means developing the ability to make personal right choices for both God and good, it is then wholesome and to be desired.* To attain this healthful balance is not easy. It must be sought prayerfully and administered in wholesome, loving relationships. A parent must know his child if he is to be able to understandingly assist in the development of freedom and inner controls.

Through personal contacts parents become the most crucial agents in the internalization of ways of living.[19] Internal and indirect controls, it is thought, are more important for boys than girls. It is possible that this is true because of the greater degree of decision-making that boys are called upon to participate in, and their more intimate and immediate contacts with society. Girls also make decisions; however, they are generally more confined and restricted in relation to the kind and intensity of decisions made because of their greater domestic involvement.

The development of inner controls for youth is also related to the development of values and convictions. The conceptions of right and wrong held by youth parallel those of their parents more than any other group of people.[20]

It has been found that young people who participate regularly in the life of the church have fewer problems of adjustment in their homes, with their friends, and in school situations than do those who take little or no part in church life.[21]

The home and the church are important agencies in relation to the formulation of both values and guiding convictions. While values are closely paralleled by conviction, their roots are much deeper. Conviction resides more on the surface and influences the formulation of lasting values. The two are almost too closely related to distinguish. Perhaps a value could be called a depth conviction. Values are not easily changed. They are formed early in life and must relate to experience in depth if they are to be changed. Convictions, on the other hand, may be classed more as surface values; not that they are less, or not important at all. They are in process of becoming a part of the life of the individual. This is why it is so important that youth, at an early age, be subjected to a wholesome environment where love, understanding, and a clear parental value system are in evidence. Youth is the period for forming clear convictions and values. They are lasting and can be changed only in the context of confidence and meaningful relationships.

Changes come and by them values and convictions are tested Change is inevitable. Youth are much more subject to change than adults. Change can be meaningful, important, and helpful if properly appropriated. Some tradition is important, for if the things which we practiced yesterday have no value today, how do we know that current practices will be worth maintaining tomorrow? It is of extreme importance that we decide where difference matters. It is necessary that, with today's youth, we build conviction concerning things that are abiding and that make a difference. It is true that as parents we may not always know where to draw the line; however, one must be drawn. The Bible must be the guide and the Christian fellowship the support for determining change. Parents and pastors in consultation with youth must determine together over the open Bible where to place boundaries.

Basic principles must be stressed such as the lordship of Jesus Christ, love, Christian stewardship and service. These are non-changing. Applications of these may change. If they do, one should not become frustrated but continually relate to the principle.

This calls for a high degree of patience and understanding. We must understand that youth are to become adults in a world that is far more alive than the world of their parents' youth. Decisions are of much broader **dimensions** and have deeper implications. The world thrown at them is alive; it is red-hot. It must be faced. Ours is the task of preparing them to handle it wisely. *Both parents and pastors need to experience prayerful searching if they are to point the way with any degree of intelligence for young people.*

Today, parents are not doing everything just as their parents did. Change is always taking place. *The basic problem is not in the change but in the quality of our faith in the unchanging Christ.*

FAITH AND DOUBT

The Bible assumes that the Christian faith is to be restorative to God, rooted in Jesus Christ, relevant to every life situation, and radiant to the world. It is also assumed that every person needs a Christ to live like, a faith to live by, a self to live with, and a cause to live for. Faith is the response of the creature to the Creator and His activity. This response then influences behavior. Paul [22] states that "faith cometh by hearing, and hearing by the word of God." The exercise of faith is not an attempt to get one to believe in something that has no ground or validity. Faith is the foundation of the Christian way of life. It is one of the spiritual laws of God. *Faith, to be meaningful, must be related to a fact and a person, the fact of the historical event, the cross, and the person of Jesus Christ who died and rose again.* Faith is a belief in the validity of a statement of fact. It is exercised daily by millions in situations and experiences that have far less validity than the Christian religion. The gift of God is eternal life. This is why faith is so important, for by faith is the gift received. It can come in no other way. Faith is the unique center of the Christian way of life. To be without it is to be lost.

It is easily understood, then, why doubt is considered serious in relation to the Christian experience. Doubt disassociates the individual from the source of grace. Doubt places distance between the Saviour and the one in need. One cannot doubt that which he has never become acquainted with or known. To know something by reason is not the same as to know something by experience. It is possible that many so-called Christians have acquired the faith that they possess on a mental basis and have never allowed it to become a living part of themselves. Faith is to be both caught and taught. It is not sufficient that it be taught only. It must be caught also. This is done in several ways. *The Christian faith is best propagated in living dynamic relationships* where individual rubs individual in living encounter. The lives that demonstrate a catching faith are consistent and deeply sincere. Faith is the most important thing in the world to such individuals. Faith can be passed on to others by association. *Seeing a father practice his belief is more important to a son than a year of sermons.* Faith must be contagious if there is to be an epidemic.

What does faith mean to the adolescent? It must be understood to be the source of strength for the Christian life. The growing adolescent, beset by inner conflicts and a searching to find his way into adult life, is in deep need of this source of strength. As far as mental development is concerned, he is in a poor position to confess this need. To youth, God often seems far away. He may be seen best through nature. A personal relationship with God is often uncertain or greatly lacking. The adolescent needs understanding in working through his searchings for God. [23] He ought not be condemned but guided. The adolescent is in the process of making many changes. One of these changes is that of making his own the religion he has been taught. The secondhand religion of his parents must become firsthand for his own personal experience. There are no easy rules to follow in relation to being certain that adolescents will come through with a strong Christian faith. The deep searching of the soul must be understood and guided to an experiential relationship with the source of the Christian faith, Jesus Christ. Christ is made real to persons through persons. To know Christ is to experience faith. To have a dynamic, relevant faith is to experience salvation. Salvation is based upon belief, not a system of "do's" and "don'ts." One may do or refrain from doing and be as lost as any man. Christianity is a religion of the heart. It cuts deeply. It involves the way people believe. Belief will undoubtedly touch actions. The Christian life is to demonstrate itself in consistent obedience.

Adolescence and youth are characterized by alternation between skepticism and belief. At about mid-adolescence, youth are usually converted or begin to seriously doubt basic Christian beliefs. Age sixteen has been referred to traditionally as the most favorable age for conversion to take place. It is probably also the most likely age for the beginning of atheistic and agnostic tendencies. [24]

While some sixteen-year-olds do not have a concept of God that is satisfying, or can't figure out what God is like, others are finding their way into a meaningful experience. Some think of God as a "person" or "figure." Most state that they don't think that God is really a man or in human form. Some think of God as Spirit, while others think of Him as "neither man nor Spirit." To many, God has become more of a guide, a ruler, a supreme being, a force, a power, or only a feeling. [25] A concept of God can be formed through religious teaching. Religion may be mishandled, with permanently damaging effect on the lives of youth. [26] One youth writes:

"I could not go to any school parties or to any ball games. It was often explained to me that we were Mennonites and we did not do the things the other kids might do. This did not set too well with me and I thought if this is what being a Mennonite means, then I want nothing to do with it. So that is how the rest of my high-school days were--no dates, no games, no parties, no social life. [27]

One of the first areas where Christian solutions must penetrate is in the area of learning. A Christian integration of all thought and life is a priority for coordinated social effort. Without this emphasis, Christian youth remain poorly prepared for the onslaughts of unbelief. [28]

Religion and psychotherapy meet in their recognition of faith as being essential to mental health. Whatever the orientation of a therapist or counselor, if he understands the problem of man, he will not deny the relevance of faith to healthy living. [29]

Americans have become more in need of conformity and belonging at the same time that they have become more associated with religion and its activities. College students follow this trend somewhat. They do, however, become less orthodox and more broad in their values. [30]

In the midst of this change, youth need to experience an integration of faith and life. A meaningful relation to Jesus Christ by faith is no accident. A passion for holiness comes as a result of an assured stand in the will of God. A healthy home and church life with a forward view concerning life and the program of Christ and the church, with ability to fit into such a program, is a sign of growth.

The level of spiritual maturity and the quality of faith in the life of an adolescent will doubtless be different from that of an adult. The maturing adolescent needs opportunity to work through doubts, to work toward a satisfactory integration of his faith, and to achieve a meaningful relationship with God. Youth need to allow the Holy Spirit the opportunity of leading them safely through their doubts. Experiences of meaningful worship, helpful discussions, service opportunities, and wholesome Christian relationships are needed to awaken youth who possess a naive, indifferent faith. They must be challenged to build a vital, meaningful faith.

It is what an adolescent believes to be true that directly influences his reactions, the actual experience having significance only indirectly, if at all. [31]

Some youth have difficulty accepting anything that does not stand the test of reason, and therefore have many doubts and a lack of faith. Belief comes through encounter. This encounter must be with living persons who know the meaning of faith and its relevance. God must open the eyes if they are to behold the true meaning of faith. Often the person who is most vocal in professing his unbelief is the one most haunted by spiritual problems. The uncertainty that comes through being divided in soul is able to produce sickness. The youth who rejects his childhood teaching, who throws away moral criteria of the past, and who wants to progress only by "reason, the yardstick, and the scales" has a desire to kill God. If this were possible, he would probably be less sick but not abounding in truth nor righteousness. [32]

The son who loves his father is right and healthy. The son who hates his father is not right but healthy. The son who loves and hates his father at the same time is neurotic.

Neurosis rests upon an inner contradiction. [33]

Many parents through inner contradictions of their own create ambivalence in youth. Extreme dogmatism or skepticism may result. A youth who is unsure may pretend to be unshakably convinced. Sometimes the most dogmatic are the weakest when the real test of faith comes.

Youth's problems must be understood. Opportunity must be given for an expansion of intellectual insight and a broadening view of the meaning of life. Freedom must also be given to make personal decisions. Youth must feel secure, wanted, and of worth. They must be involved meaningfully in the program of the church, and must relate meaningfully to others, if they are to find the way.

"So many in our churches are busy continuing something they never anywhere decisively began." [34] One does not become a Christian by assuming a secondhand faith, nor in absentia, nor by default, nor in sleep. Following Christ is a personal decision. [35] It is often those youth who come from very demanding homes and churches who seem to have the most problems with doubt. Perhaps these youth were able, for some time, to conform to the extent that their faith was not questioned. When they no longer felt these restraints, they were unable to discover the inner quality of faith that would move them from the restriction to personal experiential relationship. Where parents are inconsistent in life and practice and make demands that are beyond the understanding of youth, frustration and doubt emerge. *If a youth has been unable to relate meaningfully to father or mother, he finds it difficult to relate to God.* The Christian experience is an experience of relationships. If these relationships break down, especially in youth, it is difficult to cultivate divine relationships. One youth had much trouble believing anything related to God and the Bible. Upon investigation it was found that he had much difficulty relating to his parents. *Poor horizontal relationships hinder good vertical relationships.*

Doubt must be recognized for what it is. It must, however, be understood and worked through. Youth should not be blamed, for they are a composite of all of their experiences. Doubts which persist for a time are usually overcome when youth become involved more deeply in life and its demands. Patience, sound Christian exemplification, and understanding are necessary in helping youth from doubt to a solid core of faith in the living Christ and to a fruitful life.

The beliefs of youth today are probably no more deviant than those of their parents and grandparents when they were of similar age.

DEVELOPING PURPOSE

To be is more important than to do. Before one can do successfully, he must be. The quality of one's personhood determines the type of contribution he is able to make. God is interested in persons with self-understanding and dignity. God has a purpose for each life; it is first to be like Him, and secondly to do His will. The will of God is progressive; it is in movement within the world. We are to join with it rather than attempt to individually manipulate God into some remote individualistic program. This means that one is not only to have a proper relationship to God but also a clear understanding of himself and his purpose for living.

A survey was made to help determine where Mennonite youth are in relation to self-insight and relationships with other persons. [36] It was felt that it would be most helpful to let youth speak for themselves. They must tell us where they think they are. For the way in which a person views a situation in finality will affect his behavior and actions. The majority of these youth felt they understood themselves fairly well. Many were sometimes satisfied and sometimes dissatisfied with themselves. A majority of these youth considered themselves well adjusted. In regard to the problems which they recognized, poor relationship with parents and friends rated higher than other categories. The problem of accepting the beliefs and teachings of the church was third in order. The majority of youth felt they had a relatively happy childhood experience, with a high percent having a very happy experience. A sizable percentage felt they were receiving either some or considerable help in solving their problems. Many felt that they were receiving help through the church for problem areas. Friends and parents ranked highest in providing assistance for youth in their problem areas. Approximately one fourth felt that they were getting little or no help. Slightly less than a third felt that the church was not giving them the help that they should be getting. Many Mennonite youth appear to be turning to their friends for help in problem solving. These friends may be within or outside the church. While some youth go to parents and pastors for help, a sizable number seek it elsewhere.

This youth survey is simply saying that while in general the self-understanding and the quest for help are encouraging, there are many youth on the fringes who should give us deep concern. These are they who need special care and understanding.

Youth who understand themselves and the implication of their personal problems, and who relate meaningfully to others, are laying a foundation upon which they can build a more wholesome relationship to God. The conception that a youth has of God is often the result of either a wholesome or a warped relationship to his parents or others. If a youth is expected to be related to God in faith and love, he must previously have had experience in the same areas in his human relations. It is true also that a person cannot really know faith, love, and confidence without knowing something of their opposites. Their absence makes them of worth and desirable. This does not mean, however, that the home or church must attempt to function both as a source and as a restricting agent in the dispersing of these characteristics. Faith, love, and confidence must be demonstrated by both home and church.

In this kind of context a youth is prepared for a wholesome relation to God. God is understood in terms of his parents and church leaders, and in the context of the Christian fellowship. This means also that the value system of home and church will be more contagious. Youth must understand that they are needy and dependent and that the world is full of misrepresentations. At the same time they must experience acceptance, love, and understanding. In this context something will happen to them that is wholesome. This provides the kind of setting in which the Gospel can take on depth meaning. It provides environment for internalization of beliefs, an atmosphere for trial and error within limits, and for experiencing forgiveness and acceptance when failure or sin does occur.

Experiences of integration of faith and life toward purposeful living lead persons also to communication with others. The Gospel becomes most meaningful in living relationships. Where people rub shoulders, the practicability of the Christian experience is tested. *Personalities are formed in the context of the family to a greater degree than in any other group.* This primary group is of deep significance. While many secondary groups are also important and helpful in developing communication patterns, the home must be given credit as being the basic unit.

The adolescent in his early years is eager to experience an increasing ability to enter into meaningful interpersonal relationships. Social consciousness often expresses itself in the form of need for social approval. The adolescent is moving toward a choice for a life companion. The choice of a life vocation, which also has its religious implication, is in process of being decided. *The youth's affinity to the church is not great during this period when he is making some of life's basic decisions.* [37]

Youth's attitudes, beliefs, and behavior pattern are formed largely in and through interpersonal relationships. This may mean that all of youth's relationships need to be carefully examined. The relationship that youth should have with Jesus Christ must be the primary relationship. His relationships to parents, pastor, Sunday-school teachers, and his brothers and sisters are also very important. His relationship to his friends beyond the family group is probably the relationship of .greatest significance during the adolescent period. If all of these relationships are characterized by a deeply caring attitude, by Christian principles, and by understanding guidance, youth are experiencing an atmosphere that will contribute greatly to positive behavior. [38]

The early childhood years are considered extremely important for later development. Where love and understanding are limited by home background, they may be compensated for to a degree by present meaningful interpersonal relationships. [39]

We have attempted to look at Jesus Christ, in His relation to youth, as a model for maturation. We have sought to understand the establishing of goals and the possibility of trial and error in the life of the developing adolescent. We attempted to explore the development of inner controls. The need for the building in process of meaningful convictions was recognized. The problem of faith and doubt was explored along with a reaching for integration in one's faith experience. The development of self-insight and understanding and their relation to effective and meaningful personal relationships and one's relationship to God were explored. *It is appropriate to conclude that youth build faith in the context of living relationships charged by a strong Christian faith.*

It is appropriate yet in this chapter, by way of summary, to speak briefly to the point of the total process of maturation for all ages. Maturity is a relative experience. It is never completely realized by anyone. Regardless of age, there is always room for progression in any one area of a given individual's life. Spiritual maturity has long been sought by many. Great heroes of the faith have died seeking it. Veterans of pietistic persuasions have trudged on in hope of finding the golden path to maturity. Spiritual maturity cannot be equated with physical development. It has been said that "many well-developed bodies contain undernourished souls." One may reach his physical zenith early in life. The intellectual limits may be reached by eighteen to twenty-five years of age, but spiritual maturity is never ultimately reached here. We must await its culmination in the next world.

Having said this, however, there are general marks by which we may measure personal development in our quest for maturity. It is a temptation to measure by other persons and experiences. This is not a sufficient beginning point. It may be of help on occasions. One must always measure himself by Christ, the Christian's model for maturity. Progressive growth into His stature is the primary standard for measurement.

A second mark of maturity is the developing ability of the individual to be motivated by the love of God and a love for one's fellowmen. *Our love for God can be measured by the amount of love we possess for the individual we love least. It is possible to understand ourselves in the light of our ideals while we measure others purely on the basis of their actions.* This is not only unfair but unchristian. This kind of relationship militates against a wholesome and maturing concept of others.

A third mark of maturity is a developing ability to see all of life's experiences in a God-centered relationship. To know that God is consciously present in one's life, and Lord and master over every situation that is given to him, is a consoling factor which will aid one in his quest for maturity.

A fourth mark of maturity is a developing ability to give one's best in the cause of Christ and others. The immature would restrict the best and confine it for his own selfish impulses. The maturing individual is willing to contribute not only time and possessions but also himself for the welfare of his fellowmen.

A fifth mark of maturity is a developing ability to wait for distant goals. To the immature the immediate takes precedence and obliterates the long-range goal, which ultimately is of greatest benefit to the individual, but probably never realized because of the inability to wait patiently.

A sixth mark of maturity is a developing ability to receive love. It may usually be felt that giving love is more demanding than receiving love. In receiving love, the whole person is involved, while in giving, only a part. Receiving love demands introspection and admission of inability and dependency. Sharing admits of sufficiency and independency. While the latter is a meaningful experience, the former speaks more to the true development of a person on a spiritual level, for every man must come to a point of dependency upon God for that which man himself is unable to provide.

A seventh mark of maturity is the developing ability to feel adequate, through Christ, to each of life's demands. The demands of life are constantly increased as one moves from childhood to adult life. It is desirable that every person experience a parallel increase in personal confidence and ability to cope with the intensification of life's demands.

Some specific characteristics of maturity for youth might be summarized in the following statements:

Youth are mature to the extent that they are guided by long-term purposes rather than by close-range desires. They should be able to accept things and persons the way they are, rather than by pretending that they are as they would desire them to be. The authority of others should be accepted without rebellion. Youth should become increasingly able to accept themselves as authorities without a sense of pride or guilt. They should be able to defend themselves from their own unacceptable impulses. Ability to work without being a slave and to enter into meaningful recreation without feeling that one should be working is a mark of maturity. The maturing youth is increasingly able to accept his own and the opposite sex and the relation between the two in ways that are fulfilling. Ability to love others in such a way that one becomes less dependent upon being loved is a characteristic of maturity. One who is able to accept a significant place in the larger ongoing scheme of things and events is developing maturity. [40]

These are but a few marks of maturity that one desires to be in evidence as youth become more closely affiliated with God in the continuing quest for wholeness. *The great objective of Christian nurture is to make persons whole in Christ.*

All maturing persons should be humbly aware of imperfections and limitations and should understand that in an overarching way the grace of God must rise above all human effort to His glory.

3 NURTURE IS A PROCESS

Is nurture impossible with heredity being fixed at conception? No, environment is a second important factor in nurture. Environment may be planned throughout life. This is not to imply that heredity is not important. *This is simply to say that while heredity must be understood, it is the environment that Christian nurture is basically concerned about.*

It is important that the home, the church, and the school understand the potential of persons. Otherwise, one is shooting somewhat in the dark. Parents can make the mistake of expecting their children to enter a vocation they desire for the child or to fulfill unfulfilled ambitions of their own. Parents may, because of a desire for prestige, demand that a youth enter a certain vocation. This implies a lack of understanding. Each youth should be given careful counsel on the basis of his potential in relation to the vocation for which he feels best equipped. This means that, while heredity is fixed, it must be understood and taken into account in structuring the environment for learning.

No two persons are alike, not even in one family. The environment for learning must be flexible. It must take differences into account. Nurture must be all-inclusive. It must meet the needs of loving, growing persons.

In the development of personality both the environment and the learning content are important. Persons learn and develop their potential in the context of living relationships. This is why God sent Jesus incarnate. He could have sent a telegram. He chose to put truth in living flesh. The possibility for the same is present in the Christian home and in the church. *The environment for learning can be the most important thing that can happen to your children.* While providing for their physical well-being does consume a major block of time, the total atmosphere must be charged with a dynamic quality of relationships that supersede making the home a transit shack where clothing is changed or purchases are stored. Life is involving. Real living takes time. It is no accident. Effort must be expended in providing the quality of relationships that are more than average. The atmosphere should be charged with a quality of life and a depth of conviction that will produce values that move beyond the merely physical. The value system is formed early in life and follows rather closely that of the parents. The environment for learning is enhanced by understanding relationships. Let us explore a few of these.

LOVE AND ACCEPTANCE

To belong is like being planted, love is like rain, and communication is the cultivation.

The process of maturing allows for mistakes. When youth errs, he must be understood. Far too often parents reject both the youth and his behavior. It is more beneficial to reject the undesirable behavior while the youth continues to experience love and acceptance in spite of his errors. Even though on occasion this may be difficult, the end result will tend more to be one of meaningful relationships which will lend stability to the faltering youth.

One youth said to a counselor, "My father never admitted that he did wrong." He spoke of his father's ill-treatment of him and of the terrible beatings he received. The father would examine him at night to see if there were any open wounds. This young man, a Mennonite minister, could not understand why his own spiritual life was not meaningful and why his homelife was going backward. He found it very difficult to acknowledge mistakes. Forgiveness was not, nor had it been, a part of his family relationships. [1]

Not only forgiveness but also acceptance is important in family relationships. A person's not feeling accepted in the family will hinder his sense of acceptance by God. [2]

The parent who asks a child to forgive him for a wrong attitude is not demonstrating weakness but strength. Children must learn that their parents are not God. While parents may operate under a higher law of rightness, they are still prone to mistakes. They want and need acceptance also. Children should learn that transgression does not end the relationships they have with their parents. They should learn that transgression can provide opportunity for deeper personal relationships. [3] While sin and transgression against standards are not to be desired, if they do occur, they can be used as a learning experience. *Persons must be accepted and loved for who they are, in spite of what they are.*

Improper behavior has its roots in the experiences of children in their earliest years of life.

A youth's actions and behavior are indications of broader implications. Youth are the product of their environment. If the mother shows hostility toward the father, she may project blame upon a son by implying that he is just like his father. Or she may say to relatives or neighbors, "He has a bad tempter just like I have." When a child gets this kind of view of himself, and is punished for being like his parents, he will have difficulty understanding why behavior that is sanctioned for them is condemned for himself. [4]

It has been stated that "Nothing's improper somewhere." Propriety may be only a matter of geography. Perhaps more accurately, propriety is a matter of group boundaries, with each society possessing its own standards or patterns of action. [5]

Group standards that have become a part of a people because of a love for tradition, and have no significant value otherwise ought not be the cause of severed relationships between parents and youth, or the church and youth. Many lives have been shipwrecked because some parent or church leader was unable to make changes when needed. They were threatened by the larger group, and held acceptance by it of greater value than identity with the young person.

Youth must develop respect for persons. This includes respect for themselves and for others. Youth, while experiencing rejection by others, may at the same time be rejecting others. Fear of rejection may be expressed in many ways. Anxiety can develop concerning the finding of a meaningful place in life. Fear of not being accepted for what he is, but rather on the basis of his performance in living can cause anxiety in a youth. Youth fear the insecurity of not being loved. A lack of confidence in oneself and the development of self-respect are prevalent youth problems. The need to belong, to be assured that there is an important place in life for him, is an important concern of the adolescent. [6]

Self-rejection is common in youth and based mostly upon the inability to accept one's limitations concerning intelligence, social graces, or personal physical attractiveness. Parental hostility is not unusual in youth. This comes mainly as a result of some real or perceived restriction or mistreatment. Those who feel parents too restrictive hold a view of what they ought to be allowed to do. Some youth state they possess inferior feelings and a lack of confidence. A clear gap between what they are and what they would like to be exists. Athletics provides experiences through which a young man can develop toward his self-image. [7]

It is evident that many youth identify with someone. All youth, to develop a clear respect for persons, not only themselves, but also others, need a source of identification. In present trends toward urbanization, the father is often away from home more than with the family. This may then leave the children to identify with the man in the Western on television, the man across the street, or no man at all. Youth need associations to develop proper identity. These associations can be provided by Christian parents, pastors, and teachers. Arrangement must be made in our highly mechanized economy for our youth to maintain proper identity. Identity that is wholesome socially will aid in the development of a meaningful understanding of oneself. *If personal respect is lacking, dignity in living will also be absent.*

Environment is a modeler of persons. As a boy associates with a Christian father, his life is certain to be touched. Likewise, a girl will be deeply influenced by a Christian mother. As has been said, "The problem with many of our children is that they have parents." This implies that parents can be an influence for good or for evil. Their influence is far-reaching.

Many youth feel that the church is not filling a very significant role in meeting their problems. They feel that the church could not do much more than it is doing, however. [8]

Parents continue to be the important influence in the adolescent's life. In later adolescence many youth begin to change their former negative evaluation of their parents. [9]

Parents have a significant role in relation to the learning environment for youth. The atmosphere they provide conditions the youth in relation to his respect for both himself and other persons. The home environment provides the framework also for the acceptance of the ministry of the church to youth.

Parents and children together make up the church. Their value systems basically become the value system of the church. There must be close relationship between the two agencies. Where church and home are built upon two value systems, the youth are torn between two alternatives. The church is invariably the loser. *Home and church must work together if they expect mutual respect and loyalty.*

RELATING TO AUTHORITY

In pursuing further the environment for learning, one is confronted by the types of discipline used. In these chapters an attempt has been made to clarify the significance of the home and the church in the nurture process. We now come more directly to the patterns of authority and discipline used in each.

Many discipline patterns may be chosen, but perhaps more important than the type of discipline chosen is the degree of consistency by which the pattern is followed. *Consistency between teaching and practice in the life of the church and the family is very important.* Inconsistencies tend to break down youth loyalty to the church and to the family. Uncertainty about practices, both Biblical and cultural, is also confusing to youth. Youth tend to react against inconsistent, rigid, and harsh home, school, and church discipline patterns. They may either withdraw and cover up their feelings of resentment and aggression, or demonstrate in open acts of rebellion against parents, the church, or the community. [10] One youth who seemed well adjusted and obedient expressed with tears her resentment and ill feelings toward a harsh domineering father. Outward appearance may never reflect inner conflict.

Mennonites have emphasized pure and consistent living along

with right thinking.[11] The reactions of many youth seem to be saying to us that it is high time that we adults stop practices for the purpose of prestige or position. They want adults to cease to be men-pleasers. They want them to find the values of the Gospel that are lasting, and consistently practice them. If parents want to build within youth appreciation for truths that are lasting, they must be able to draw a clear line between the important and the unimportant. *Too long parents have tied tradition to theology and made them of like importance.* It is now time to distinguish between the two. Even though a tradition may continue as a practice, it must be understood to be such and, perhaps no more than a kind of vehicle used to convey some meaning that might be conveyed in other ways.

Consistency is a jewel. It is priceless. It is difficult to attain but of lasting value where practiced.

Inconsistency in discipline patterns seems to be a factor associated quite closely with feelings of jealousy. Mother is the one person most important in relation to the development of social behavior.[12] This means that consistency in her life is of great importance in the life of the child, and is evidently where consistency counts most strongly. In one study parental behavior, especially that of the mother, appeared to be most significantly related to the personality development of adolescent boys living in the city; parental conduct seemed less important for those boys living on farms or in small towns. It is felt that relationship of parents to girls is not as important as for boys.[13]

Parents have difficulty expressing consistent consistency. The parent may be a different person in the family than he is to his employer. There may be so much contrast that one is afraid to let the people in one group know how he behaves in another. One's different selves may be in conflict.[14] Sooner or later this conflict may be evidenced in all relationships.

Youth require consistency more than adults. If it is lacking, a part of their needed support is missing. Values will be ill-formed and personality will be warped if inconsistency persists.

Both homes and churches must give themselves to consistent living so that it will be possible for youth to find the way in value formation. Where consistency is lacking, love, if present, may compensate to a degree and bridge the youth over the inconsistencies. *Homes and churches that demonstrate a high degree of consistency tend to develop youth who are more mature in both personality and behavior.*

Not only is the element of consistency an important factor, but the type and intensity of discipline is basic for wholesome nurture.

All youth face the problem of understanding the meaning of authority and freedom. A youth early in life develops certain attitudes toward the authority of his parents, the church, the community, and the state. Many times he views authority as that element that keeps him from getting what he wants. He views freedom as being free from parents, or other organizations, to be able to do as he pleases. In his attempt to find freedom he sees all authority relationships as a threat. He attempts to run his own life, not do what his parents desire, or what others may think best. The person who uses this avenue of operation is stopping short of a meaningful understanding of relationships, dependency, freedom, authority, mutuality, which are very necessary for meaningful living. [15]

The less authoritarian family pattern is beneficial for the development of desirable personality traits in children. Some researchers see in the modern democratic companionship family strengths that are lacking in the traditional patriarchal family. [16]

The more direct and inconsistent the discipline in both the home and the church, the more likely youth are to leave home and marry at a premature age. Where the discipline is consistent and less authoritarian, youth attend church with a greater degree of regularity. The ages when youth become members of the church are less extreme in this kind of atmosphere. Conversion experiences tend to be more satisfying under a consistent and less authoritarian atmosphere. Where the home is authoritarian and inconsistent, parents have less opportunity to lead their children to salvation. This is more often done by an evangelist. *Personality development of youth from authoritarian and inconsistent homes tends to be lower and the behavior less desirable.* [17]

Authority and discipline do not represent only unpleasant areas of a youth's life. On many occasions a youth depends upon the authority of an adult. He seeks not only freedom from the adult but his control as well. Even though youth may rebel against control they would feel lost without it. They want to be free and yet seek direction. They are slow, however, to admit this need. [18]

Methods of discipline have changed much in past years. The trend today is toward more leniency and less physical punishment. To gain obedience some mothers use severe corporal punishment, others unfavorable comparisons; some nag, bribe, bargain, or use many other methods. Whatever the method used, the primary distinction in relation to the effect upon the child is whether the method is consistent or inconsistent. [19]

The philosophy of the past generation was obedience for its own sake. A number of youth reported that their parents seldom or never explained punishment. Affection for parents plays a major role in the control of deviant behavior. Many youth who sense a close relationship to parents do not want to hurt them. This kind of relationship is a controlling factor in behavior. While ultimately the stimulation should be something other than praise or non-severing of ties, these aspects are beneficial for encouraging right action. [20]

Youth of this generation have difficulty in identification because there is so little to identify with. "They are a little like someone who comes to a **Grange** supper and would like to help, except that there is nothing more to do: everything is all set." [21]

Youth need understanding, consistent parents, with which to identify. Parents must use discipline, train Godward, guide effectively, with understanding care. Where some parents tend to be over-indulgent, others prefer harshness. They believe that an assault on a youth will **strengthen him and lead to self-discipline**. [22]

Parents may use many methods of discipline. They may range from a tongue lashing to playing the martyr role, or to comparison **of age difference. Most of these** can be an injustice to a youth because they incur undue guilt, arouse anxiety or fear, or weaken the personality. None of these are fair. [23]

"You can punish any child you have the right and strength to punish. You can only discipline those children who make them-selves your disciples." [24]

3

The democratic family, like the democratic marriage, should be characterized by unity, togetherness, and self-realization. [25]

Aggression by youth is threatening. Many feel it calls for discipline. Usually permissiveness leads to aggression. Aggressiveness must be guided. In both home and church, there is a need for youth who have been guided into wholesome growth and development by the loving, understanding care of parents and church leaders who were neither too strict nor too lenient. Youth need to associate with persons who, through the leadership of the Spirit, find the way into meaningful growth and development.

The home is a most crucial factor in determining the attitudes, beliefs, and behavior pattern of youth. The quality of husband-wife relationships is also deeply important. The control pattern and the level of affection among family members are very significant. *The quality of the child's relationship to his parents is influential in determining whether he will accept the social and spiritual standards which his parents teach.* The mental and emotional distance between parents and children is often great. It is difficult, once these distances emerge, for either parent or child to make the accepted move in bridging such gaps. [26]

Evidence indicates that the more democratically structured family obtains better interpersonal relationships between husband and wife, and parents and children, than the families in which the authority tends to be too centered in the family head. In families where authority is shared, the emotional climate rates higher. Related to good emotional climate is a high level of affection and a discipline system that is effectively administered in such a way that the child perceives freedom rather than restriction in his relationship to his parents. [27]

Some Christians feel that growth takes place by talking words to people. This is far too automatic. [28] Meaningful learning is more than a result of words. *Religion that is meaningful is taught by relationships and words.* Christian nurture must understand the place of authority and discipline in the learning process. Authority and discipline are a means and not an end. *Meaningful discipline understands and relates persons to truth in the context of loving concern.*

ATTITUDES AND BEHAVIOR

An attitude may be defined as an emotionally charged response to a stimulus. The question might be asked, Which comes first, an attitude, a perception, a value, or an understanding? It seems that one first perceives, then an understanding is formulated and an attitude emerges, which **then** flavors the value system. The attitude which may be more emotionally charged than any of the other elements may influence greatly the behavior of persons.

Basically, *attitudes are caught and not taught*. Inconsistencies in youth may stem from inconsistencies of parents. Attitudes of parents toward local government, race, authority, and money influence those of youth. All of these areas are important, and are related to the attitudes and behavior patterns of youth. [29]

Attitudes are formed in the context of home, church, and community life. Many intense attitudes may be formed because of negative reaction to authoritarianism. This is evident in parent-child relationships.

One youth reports:

Sometimes when our folks told us to do something and we would ask why, they would say, "Just because I said so." This would just burn me up on the inside. . . . Whenever Dad was fixing something, he made us boys run after anything he needed. We would walk and then he would yell at us and tell us to run. If we couldn't find it as fast as he thought we should, he would yell and come after it. If he would find it, he would then bawl us out for not looking very well. This would make me mad inside. [30]

When a youth is not considered as an individual in his own rights and demands are made that are not appropriate, or, not explained even if they are appropriate, something happens to the youth inside.

One boy claimed as a college youth that he could not attend chapel or church worship because he could not bear to listen to the reading of the Bible. His father, it was found, had required him to memorize a verse of Scripture before he could have breakfast. Some of the verses were so long and so hard and he was so hungry that he literally came to hate the Book from which they came. [31]

A father with the best intentions and the best material can produce antagonistic results. One wise parent said, *"Adultism is the rock of offense in childhood."*

The more extreme an attitude, the more intensely it is likely to be held. Some attitudes may be more strongly held by people who are on the defensive and opposed to a change of old norms. There is a tendency for older people to hold their attitudes with greater intensity than youth. [32]

The goal should be to develop the capacity to express our various inner drives in a way that is self-satisfying. Consideration of others must also be taken into account, as well as our own accepted goals which reach beyond ourselves as individuals. [33] This means that in the formulation of attitudes, selfishness must not be the guiding factor. Improper attitudes toward the church and church leaders can reflect nothing but selfish motivation. These attitudes are then picked up by youth and flavor the formulation of their own value system.

There are several kinds of attitudes: attitudes that are highly charged with emotion and attitudes that are well seasoned, deliberate, and wholesome. The environment is responsible for attitudes and attitudes affect values and behavior. *Homes and churches must major in the development of Christian attitudes and behavior.*

Prejudice is closely related to attitudes and attitude formation. A prejudice may result from a highly emotional situation. This kind of situation may or may not be founded upon right thinking. Prejudice is an attitude flavored by strongly biased ideas or action.

A child is usually expected to acquire his parents' loyalties and prejudices. If the parent because of his particular group membership is an object of prejudice, the child is more or less victimized. [34]

Highly prejudiced youth believe that there is only one right way to do a thing. They feel that they must watch every move or someone will take advantage of them. They believe that control should be more strict. They also feel that only people who are like themselves have a right to be happy. [35] In the case of highly prejudiced youth, insecurity seems to lie at the root of the personality. [36] Prejudiced people require clear-cut structure in their world even if it is narrow and inadequate. [37] Research shows that prej-

udiced people are more devoted to institutions than are unprej-
udiced people.[38] Prejudiced people may therefore feel more secure
within a church that has a structural program that experiences
little alteration. A prejudiced person distrusts people until they
prove themselves trustworthy. The essential philosophy of a democratic atmosphere is exactly the opposite. Democracy trusts a
person until he proves himself untrustworthy.[39] Prejudiced people
desire law and order. Their lives feel safer where strict rules are
imposed.[40]

There is evidence that tolerant people are more accurate in
their judgment of personalities than prejudiced people.[41]

The family can be and is one of the most influential factors
in developing tolerance. Later experience, without a doubt, is
also important. However, the family is the basic factor in producing
a tolerant personality. Other forces that have their influence are
school and community experiences.

Religion tends both to increase and to decrease prejudice
depending on how the individual views his religion.[42] As long
as there are individuals with different central values, there will
be disagreement. Those people who argue violently for or even
die for their views may not necessarily be the victims of prejudice.[43]
However, if one is given to flavoring ethnic prejudice with religious
sanction, trouble emerges.[44] Conviction and prejudice differ. Prejudice may have religious connotations as well as conviction. The
major difference seems to be in the foundation upon which each
rests. Prejudice is highly opinionated while conviction is built upon
truth. It has been said that *"a man may push an opinion but
conviction will drive a man."*

A democratic and tolerant person is not necessarily Christian.
Many democratic personalities, to be sure, are not religious in
character.[45] A democratic atmosphere simply is the kind of atmosphere that provides for understanding relationships in a Christian
context. It does not in any way preclude discipline. It simply calls
for discipline in an understanding relationship. A democratic environment does not necessarily find its depth in tolerance. By toleration
is meant an understanding relationship where there is communication between persons with recognition of individual personalities.

Prejudice develops in a family setting where a relationship of authority rather than love prevails. [46] Prejudice disturbs human relations because it has its roots in insecurity. [47] The end result that is desired in the life of youth is the development of understanding behavior. While spiritual life and growth cannot be measured alone by behavior, youth's conduct assists in determining the effect of nurture.

Behavior cannot be predicted by norms because no one ever continuously conforms to a norm. [48] Behavior is dynamic; it fluctuates. Behavior is caused; it is purposeful; it is usually the result of some basic reason. [49] Behavior is difficult to measure. It is fluid, and is continually in a state of change. [50] One must be able to understand the cause of behavior if he is to be helpful. To punish only for the act is insufficient; one must also attempt to determine the motivation. Persons differ greatly. A type of behavior coming from one person at a given time may be appropriate while the same behavior from another person at another time may be inappropriate. The age, the level of maturation, as well as other factors, must be given consideration.

When parents fail to understand, the child is apt to feel hurt, rejected, displeased, or frustrated. If his good behavior is not satisfactorily rewarded, in protest the child may resort to defensive behavior. By this method he's attempting to punish his parents because they have hurt him. If his good behavior has been ignored, he discovers that he can at least get attention, even if the attention is in the form of punishment, by engaging in parentally disapproved behavior. In this kind of relationship a cycle is set up in which the parent fails to show adequate love and the child reacts in strong protest. The parents then punish the child for his reaction and the child's love becomes less in the process. This cycle must be broken, else behavior results which will be embarrassing to both parent and child. If this kind of relationship exists, the parent often increases his control or discipline pattern, pushing the child to several alternatives. He may inhibit his feelings and withdraw, trying to avoid displeasure by avoiding his parents altogether; or he can continually express his protests by rebellious behavior. By adolescence this experience may develop into a kind of warfare not only with his parents but also with teachers, pastors, or other authority figures. Wise parents will remain open to signs which may indicate this kind of trend.[51]

A pattern of resistance to parental authority can be transferred to other persons of authority such as God, the minister, or a youth's teachers.

Behavior and conduct are often emotional rather than ideational[52] A youth responds on the basis of the way in which he perceives a situation to be rather than as it is. It is his perception of the situation that causes his desirable or undesirable behavior.

Behavior is a result of relationships. It has been found that inconsistent and overly strict discipline does detriment to behavior, while on the other hand too little control may not give the desired direction to behavior. The atmosphere that is most conducive to wholesome behavior is the situation in which there is love for persons in spite of activity. Where personality is not threatened but allowed to develop, and where there is acceptance for what a person is, relationships of love can produce desirable behavior. *Good, desirable behavior is no accident. Christian family relationships must prevail and take precedence over all other responsibilities if children are to grow up unto the Lord in all things.*

THE LEADERSHIP PROBLEM

Unchristian attitudes and behavior may be related to the quality and distance of parent-child, laity-ministry relationships.

Youth are not the only factor in the interpersonal relationship experience. Parents and pastors are important persons.

Parents may have the problem of uncertainty about leadership tasks. With the shift from more parent-centered to more group-centered family patterns, confusion and misunderstanding about the respective duties of both husband and wife have resulted. The wife may assume the task of income earner as well as business manager. Husbands, especially when the wife is working, may take on a more feminine role. Tensions may develop when the expectations of husband and wife are too demanding.

There is also the problem of shared authority in the home. Traditionally the father assumed the task of disciplinarian. If the husband has come up through this kind of environment and the wife has come up through a more democratic structure, problems may result.

Husbands and wives need a clear communication pattern about leadership duties. A clear understanding is essential for the maintenance of good home environment.

Another problem is in relation to the amount of control children should be subjected to in the family. There is much variation relative to both theory and practice. Psychologists through research have proposed that *the more democratic family structure is conducive to better and more desirable personality characteristics.* The authoritarian atmosphere tends to restrict both personality development and desirable behavior. Where one parent has been brought up under one system and the other parent under the opposite, understanding will need to emerge in relation to the discipline pattern. Consistency must be maintained if parents desire wholeness in the personality of their children.

The result of the absence of parents from the home is also a factor for concern. Farming involved the whole family. Today, with many parents involved in vocations beyond the home, and with both parents on the job, children are left more to themselves or to a so-called "sitter." This kind of continued relationship is a threat to the emotional well-being of the children not completely compensated for by the additional financial facility.

Unchristian behavior is more likely to occur when youth are away from their parents than when they are with them.

Whether the wife should work outside the home is often a point of contention. This should be carefully looked at both by the parents and by the children who are old enough to share in relation to the validity of such a plan.

An additional leadership problem deals with pressures on family life from the outside. With increased communication and transportation and more highly economized relationships, all family members, as soon as they are old enough to move beyond homelife, are thrown into a world of different ideas and ideals. The question is, "Can the home maintain its strength to support spiritually the youth who come and go from its shelter?"

The Mennonite Church has in recent years turned toward parochial education on the elementary level. This places additional financial burden upon some families. Where this takes the mother from the home, for work, to pay the tuition, the question can be asked whether the problem her absence creates in the home is compensated for by the Christian education. *The need today is for parents, as spiritual leaders, to provide the kind of environment that will internalize values and controls to the extent that youth will be able to stand alone in a world that threatens Christian principles.*

Parents also face the problem of making relevant the doctrine of nonresistance and the way of love in all family relationships. Love must mean more than taking good care of a child physically. Can the doctrine of "spare the rod and spoil the child" be harmonized with the New Testament teaching of love? It is questionable whether the father who faithfully provides for his children physically, while at the same time depriving them of his companionship, loves his children. True love must be communicated by parents not only in providing for but in sharing oneself with the family. [53]

It has been suggested that the greater the feeling of failure in achieving a life goal that is important to a parent, the greater will be the desire for children. Where parents have failed to achieve, families may have become large. There is then less time for each child. It has also been suggested that a greater than average desire for children will be linked with a greater than average need to prove one's adequacy in terms of knowledge and power, sexual competence, and the ability to love. A less than average desire for children may be associated with a greater than average fear of yielding a dependent position. [54]

Most parents who have difficulty bringing up their children may also themselves be struggling with problems of adjustment, and may be to a mild or severe degree themselves neurotic. [55]

Parents should be cautious not to place the blame for their own problems upon the backs of their children.

The firstborn is the one on whom parents displace feelings of strongest conflict. Children in a family may be the recipients of the parents' feeling of love, hostility, guilt, anxiety, or ambition.

To reject a child infrequently and mildly, is not serious. It is the total balance of love and hate that counts and not the isolated incidental expressions of either. Neglect and deprivation may have more lasting effects upon a child than threats and overdrawn punishment. [56]

Not only do parents have problems in relation to the role they are to play within the family, and concerning their relationship with their children, but pastors and other group leaders as well have problems.

A basic leadership problem is found in being more concerned about principles, rules, and standards than persons. Living persons should be the basic concern of each leader. The growth and development of the personality and the interpersonal relationships that influence persons are factors that should influence the behavior of every leader. To carefully maintain a standard at the expense of youth within the church is unwise. The youth must develop into maturity and learn to relate to wholesome demands. The problem of bringing the two together remains as the challenge.

A second problem many leaders in the church face is the problem of position and overlapping membership. Demands are made either to gain good standing or to maintain a position within a hierarchy, rather than practicing a real love for and an understanding of people. A leader may constantly be attempting to please some other group. If his standards, either real or perceived, are not maintained, a barrier can be erected which cuts off further communication with his people.

A third problem deals with the leader's understanding of the church and the task of the laity. He may visualize the church as "his" church where the people are all to follow, without seriously thinking, the pattern that he and God set. He forgets that God may also speak through the laity to reveal His will. The laity are to be the cutting edge of the church. They are to be individuals in society where actual living dialogue takes place.

All ministers must remember that they were one time laymen. The ministry is chosen to represent and serve the lay membership. Both ministers and laity are the church and not the ministry alone.

Standards that a group sets for itself will be more realistic, more attainable, and more comfortable than standards that are imposed upon it from the outside. Furthermore, when persons within a group have a hand in setting their own standards, they are much more likely to accept and follow those standards. The standards that a group sets are often much higher than those set by external authority. [57]

The group must be involved in setting standards. Many leaders, like Moses, burden themselves unduly. *Responsibility needs to be passed "out" rather than "down" so that all may feel an equal sense of responsibility.*

Youth are concerned about unclear goals found among parents and pastors. They want to know what is right and do it. They need the kind of guidance that makes sense.

The majority of our youth in the church are earnest Christians and compare favorably with the youth of other churches. Concern is appropriate, however, for the sizable minority that appear to be somewhat indifferent and weak in spiritual understandings and in Christian witness. A small group show defiance toward the church, indifference to Christ, and a behavior pattern of a somewhat serious nature. [58]

A challenge to both parents and church leaders is the fringe group. The church has, through the past decades, lost hundreds of youth to other churches or to no church at all, often because of faulty leadership. The challenge is to know and understand each youth and attempt to meet his personal need early in life, giving him guidance to become what he ought to be.

Mennonite youth tend to have definite opinions as to how their parents and pastors feel toward them. *In seeking counsel for their problems, Mennonite youth turn most often to their friends, secondly to their parents, and last to their pastor.* [59] This is an indication of a lack of relationship where it should be strong. It may also be an indication of authoritarian leadership, for autocracy militates against wholesome interpersonal relationships.

It is time for both pastors and parents to evaluate their communication patterns and explore new channels for communication. Church leaders need to explore new possibilities of leadership. If leaders of the church are not cautious, they may be flockless leaders.

They might need to comment as did Gandhi, "There go my people; I must follow them, for I am their leader."

Group members tend to relate to others in the same way they perceive the group leader relating to them. It is the leader's task to attend to the needs of others, understand meanings and intents, convey a spirit of acceptance, and link together persons by molding and shaping ideas. [60]

The spirit of the leader is a large factor in both home and church. *The crying need of the hour is for consecrated parents and pastors who will take seriously the job of building persons. This kind of building is the only kind with eternal dimensions. We must build well.*

BELIEF AND PRACTICE

One of the greatest goals in relation to youth work for parents, pastors, and youth leaders is the building in of a clear set of values. For youth to journey through life, rub shoulders with folks who are responsible for their eternal well-being, and sense no unique set of clear values, is a shame. *We owe our youth clarity and purpose.*

Values are acquired early in life and are not easily changed. An attempt at changing values once acquired can be very threatening. The result can be an inner war in the life of a youth. Few people can assist; he must work through this conflict on his own. The time to give meaningful assistance is when the value system is being formed.

Parents' value systems are of crucial importance. The parent who has a clear value system and high standards is a reservoir of strength to the youth confronted by conflicting standards and practices. [61] The home atmosphere may advance or hinder the adolescent's aspirations to achieve adulthood. [62]

When core values conflict and when persons choose values that are contrary to each other, there will be continued emotional conflicts and maladjustment. [63]

Acceptance of Mennonite values by Mennonite youth, and desirable personal and social development, are influenced by the type, degree, and consistency of discipline used in both the home and the church. The acceptance of Mennonite values by youth is also greatly influenced by the degree of acceptance of the same values by the parents, and by the affectional quality of the relationship between the parents and youth. [64]

Parents need to see the importance of being genuinely Christian. They must understand the importance of family harmony, the value of a relaxed and pleasant atmosphere in the home, and the kind of situations that lead youth to accept their values. Parents must develop a positive attitude toward Christianity and the church. To do this they must demonstrate love in all their relationships. Acceptance and forgiveness must be demonstrated before all their children. They must live by the standards which they profess to hold. They must recognize that their children need to be treated as real persons at all age levels. [65]

The church needs to recognize the importance of winning the love, respect, and confidence of its youth. Stress should be placed upon love, goodwill, and confidence on the part of ministers and teachers toward youth. Care should be taken to preach the Word of God in completeness. The reality of sin, the remedy of the Gospel, grace and forgiveness, the nature of the Christian life, the role of the Holy Spirit, the significance of prayer, and the value of Christian unity should all be reoccurring themes in the life of the congregation. [66]

Youth must learn respect for their parents, the church, and the community. While they suddenly learn that all persons are human and make mistakes, they too must learn the forgiveness and grace of God and its implications for the acceptance of all persons. They must learn that being Christian calls for principles that differ from those of sub-Christian society. They must learn that a lifetime of happiness may depend upon their ability to make wise choices in their youth. They must learn, too, that patience and understanding are important virtues in relation to the older generation. [67]

A youth at times may face conflict as to whether he is to follow his religious values, or the standards of his friends and maintain their approval. Some evidence points to the fact that many youth do not rely on religious resources when faced with moral choices. [68]

The expediency of the decision of the moment seems most important.

Youth must make choices. The equipment that is given them during childhood and early adolescence will be that with which they must work in youth. In the nurture process standards must be set. They will need to be consistent and well explained. Youth need boundaries. They do not care to have these boundaries imposed upon them but feel insecure when they are removed. *Youth need and like counsel. They do not care to admit it, however. They want to know that an adult who cares and knows is near. They want the adult to be a resource person when needed, but not to impose his ideas upon them.*

By the time of adolescence most youth have formed their value system. This has become the result of years of exposure to adults and other youth. To change it is like pulling teeth. There must be a very dynamic environment if values are to be changed at all. When this does take place, caution must be exercised in relation to maintaining the integrity of the individual. The changing of values can best take place in the context of a group. Group therapy is helpful in leading individuals to change behavior. Behavior can best be changed by teaching in the context of discussion. Where individuals with like needs, like goals, but differing behavior meet, the influence one can have upon the other is alarming. This is why it is important that the environment be so structured that the positive influence will weigh more heavily than the negative. The right choice of persons, the proper curriculum materials, and the environment are all important.

Group therapy is a relatively new process of changing values and behavior. Its potential is not completely explored. So far its practice has proved helpful in many groups. Its value for the church could be great. It remains to be seen what can be done through this kind of experience for youth. Medical doctors, Christian youth, community leaders, ministers, parents, teachers, and others may all exert helpful influence in group discussions.

Both the home and the church must major on the integration of belief and practice. Parents are the first agents who have opportunity to make this relationship understandable. Their opportunity begins in the child's early years. Later on, other agencies take over.

The three outstanding hindrances to spiritual growth in youth are unchristian associations, church beliefs, and parental relationships. This is the order of influence.[69] In adolescence the friends one chooses take over and may exert influence either for good or for ill. Neither the parents nor the church are among the best sources of help in meeting adolescents' needs. Either the help of the friends one chooses or their working through issues on their own forms the adolescent pattern. This means that *if the home has done its earlier job well, the adolescent will be better able to make wise choices and meaningful decisions.*

The home and the church must always stand ready to provide opportunity for the meeting of youth's needs. They cannot, however, force help upon them. They must simply be available. The church can and must provide a strong program of Christian education and group activities for the integration of belief and practice. Unless the home and the church have demonstrated a consistent and meaningful pattern of life, youth will be at sea.

The environment for learning is of basic importance in the nurture process. The responsibility for nurture goes more deeply than providing good curriculum materials, as helpful as they may be. It also goes beyond the providing of good elementary and secondary schools. The responsibility moves back to the home as the first agent and to the church as the second agent in the process of developing persons who will be able to live as Christian disciples.

It is natural for youth to have personal frustrations, to encounter doubt, and to experience some degree of rebellion. The task of both home and church is to provide the kind of environment that will help them to realistically face all of these issues and come through the better for having done so. Youth may always have a core of unresolved issues. This is normal. If the number of unresolved issues overshadows the number of resolved issues, frustration may result which can unbalance the seeking youth.

Youth are called to develop Christian personality in the midst of a depersonalized society. Where the trend is in favor of lack of personal responsibility and free living, we must help youth find the true value of Christianity.

When adults find a sense of worth, dignity, and purpose, this then becomes an added stimulation to youth toward wholesome achievement. Nurture then takes on an added dimension because one is nurturing not only for the present but also for eternity. Nurture must involve preparation for both the present and the future. It must assist individuals to discriminate between the valuable and the valueless. It must help people take sides not for contention but for progress. Life is decisive. It is involving. *The decisions that are made in youth can give guidance to the remainder of one's life. This is why nurture in a living context is extremely important.*

4 RELATIONSHIPS AFFECT GROWTH

Relationships are the context into which individuals are thrust. The quality of these relationships is a determining factor in the process of nurture. It is most appropriate to explore a number of these relationships so that a sense of direction might be attained concerning the implications of their influence upon spiritual growth and development.

All lives become a part of each other through personal contact. To choose associates wisely is like being a skilled mason.

PERSONAL UNDERSTANDING

To know one's self is the greatest of insights. Favorable attitudes toward God and the church are more likely to exist within the youth who has a clear understanding of himself.

Changes in development take place rapidly. The chief difference between adolescence and other periods of life is that things happen so quickly in relation to physical development. A fast process of change is more stressful to the physical and mental balance of youth than a slow process. Stress and strain are to be expected during youth's developing experiences. [1]

Physical factors are influential and must be seen in relation to all other factors in the nurture process. Some physical changes which alter a youth's view of himself are increase in height and weight, changes in proportion and contour of the body, and the changes on the body surface in relation to skin and hair. There are also changes in experiences of the body. The voice changes, the appetite increases, there is more strength and energy, and a new experience of sexuality, including feeling and function, emerges. There are also changes in relation to former associations when puberty occurs. These changes may be within the same sex group or between the sexes. [2]

During puberty girls develop faster than boys. A thirteen-year-old girl is usually much more of a woman than a thirteen-year-old boy is a man. [3]

The image a youth has of himself physically has a close relationship to the image he has of himself as a person. The feelings a youth has about himself are deeply embedded in the understandings he gains through experiencing his own body. [4]

Defects, blemishes, and scars all have influence in relation to personality development. Some of these cannot be altered. Where it is possible for correction to be made, parents ought to give assistance for such change. Where defects are incurable, the youth should be accepted as a person and never made the target of ridicule or jokes. Individuals are sensitive about their bodies. They are theirs; they must live in them all through life. They must know them, understand them, and admire them. The physical body is so close to a person that it tremendously affects the development of personality.

The increase in growth rate followed by the attainment of sexual maturity is regarded as the chief characteristic of youth. The physical mechanism upon which these changes are based has received little attention. [5]

One basic factor in development that must be taken into account is the difference in sexes. It has already been stated that girls mature earlier than boys. In addition, it is quite clearly understood that blood pressure, respiratory volume, and metabolism change very much at puberty and differ significantly between boys and girls. The differences between physical and emotional characteristics are well known. These differences can create great handicaps and social problems for the adolescent. [6]

Another problem is the timetable for maturity. Seldom do two adolescents mature at the same rate. One girl may be very mature at thirteen while her friend may not have begun to develop many adult characteristics. [7]

Youth face many problems in relation to adjustment to a new body. A major task of adolescence is the adjustment needed in relation to the dramatic physical changes which mark the movement of the child into adulthood. [8]

The body, the self, and society are in constant interaction and no one of these can be understood apart from the other two. The physical functions serve as a background against which the other two factors interact increasingly. The culture and self may play the greatest role, while the physical dimension serves as a center. [9]

Biological factors affect the overall possibilities of healthy personal development. The nervous system, gland functioning and balance, drives and urges, and stress and strain arising from body changes all leave an imprint.

Youth's emotional, behavioral, and spiritual problems can be a natural result of physical maturation and developmental characteristics. The need for independence, the struggle for self-identity, the desire for companionship with the opposite sex, and conflicting values between the generations are particular needs made evident as youth develop. [10]

While the physical developmental changes do not explain youth's behavior, completely, it is assumed that their behavior cannot be explained without taking the physiological changes into account as a starting point. [11]

It should not be assumed that individuals are the victims of their heredity alone, but it must be understood that heredity does have a major part to play in the kind of person that emerges in later life.

Each youth is different. His heredity, while similar to his brother's and sister's, is unique. There is no one exactly like him. He must be understood for who he is and what he has to offer. He is not to be blamed for those things which he cannot change. He must be accepted for who he is and understood to be an individual in his own rights. To do less than this is to injure personality. Often this injury occurs in childhood and leaves its marks on adult life. The child with teeth that are less than perfect, with facial blemishes, deformed limbs, or with looks that are less desirable must be accepted. These characteristics can have an effect upon his personality. This is why acceptance is so important.

Appropriate relationships with the opposite sex need to be

provided or allowed at the appropriate time. This is normal and must be understood to be a part of the process of normal maturation.

The early maturing girl naturally has an interest in boys. Her social interests may be much broader than those of her age mates. The boys of her age-group may be unreceptive. While she may be a year or two out of step with the girls in her class, she may be three or four years out of step with the boys of her age. This is a terrifying degree of developmental difference. [12]

Relationships with the opposite sex are conditioned not only by physical development but also by the relationship of the child to the family setting. Where boys are closely attached to the mother, progress in courtship is slow. Girls who are closely attached to their father find progress easy in courtship. The absence of a father in the home makes courtship progress for boys difficult. The absence of either parent seems to make no difference in courtship experiences for girls.

Children who show a preference for one parent usually prefer mother. At times boys will prefer their mother, while girls will have a preference for their father. Mothers tend to prefer their sons, and fathers their daughters. Parents often prefer sons to daughters. [13]

Both the physical development and the home atmosphere help in determining progress in the social life of youth. While the physical developmental process cannot be given credit for all the problems or meaningful experiences, it must be understood for what it is and what it means in the life of youth.

Parents are responsible to plan the kind of environment that will lend itself to the wholesome development of the adolescent. The chief concern of parents should be their child or children and their welfare. All other activities should be relegated to second place. All remunerative pursuits should be followed not as an end in themselves, but as a means to the end of raising a family for Christ and the church. To provide the proper environment may at times mean a physical move from one geographical region to another. It may mean changing the educational possibilities of the child. It could even mean the change of church home if the present congregation is not meeting the spiritual needs of the adolescent.

Parents are the God-ordained guides of youth. They are trusted with the care of a soul for which to plan responsibly. It is much better to send a youth into the world with proper social, spiritual, emotional, and mental equipment, than to send him forth with a new car, new clothing, and a bank account. A youth's appearance may be well cared for, but he may be completely unprepared to face the issues of life. One cannot bluff nor buy his way into maturity. A child carries out from his home exactly what his parents give him.

Even the best homes may face tensions. These experiences should not be discouraging. They will come. The home that is a citadel of faith will provide security to weather the greatest stress. Real problems face those homes which have a shallow faith, little security, and a lack of love. During stress and tension, they have insufficient resources with which to meet the demands. A strong faith in the lordship of Christ for each family member is a requirement for facing life and its tensions.

Change creates tension. Not all tension is undesirable. If tension exists between the youth and Christ, help needs to be given in allowing Christ to become the Lord of his life. If tension exists between a youth and the world, this is more desirable. He must, however, understand that the world is to be lived in and cannot be ignored. *The world need not pipe the tunes by which youth dance. The world need not call the plays of life's great game.*

The potential of youth must be guided into channels of usefulness. Relationships exist; they cannot be bypassed. It is how individuals relate and to what they relate that makes the difference.

With proper spiritual relationships, both with the Christ who bought them and their parents who taught them, youth can move into the world to face confusion and unrest with spiritual poise and confidence.

RELATING TO THE FAMILY

The relationships of family members, parents with children, children with children, and parent with parent are of extreme importance. It is on the basis of relationships that personality patterns are developed.

There are many aspects of human relations. There are many factors influencing these relationships. Retention of family loyalty, overlapping group membership, or some fantasy in relation to unfulfilled desires can influence relationships tremendously. Relationships are so important that they need to be carefully understood and analyzed. It is often difficult for parents to take an objective look at inner-family relationships because they are so deeply involved. Sometimes outside help is needed when relationships become tense and impenetrable. The pastor should always be available to give understanding help in such cases.

Tensions may arise in the family from a number of sources. Religion and religious practices are often a first cause for tension. The family that professes no religion may have fewer tensions; however, their quality of life may be much lower. Many parents who profess religion have a tendency to raise standards. In their pursuit of perfection many family members become frustrated.

Cultural factors are also a point of tension because they often take on religious implications.

There has been a shift from an authoritarian pattern toward a less authoritarian pattern in discipline. Tensions are created between youth and parents because youth tend to accept the less authoritarian pattern more easily. A conflict may arise in the adolescent's mind over the inconsistent uses of discipline for obtaining his conformity to a way of life encouraged for adults. [14]

Social institutions establish norms of conduct or rules for all individuals who are participants in them. The primary norms for parents in the American family are affection and authority. For youth they are respect, obedience, and the return of affection. The effectual role of the parent has been strengthened as an ideal due to the growth of individualism and an increased knowledge of child psychology. [15] It is a recognized fact that *affection is the first essential to the wholesome personality development of the child.* [16] The quality of parent-child relationships may vary directly with the frequency of the child's interaction with parents in activities of work or play. [17]

Authoritarianism will appear to be a problem to youth in direct relation to the degree to which parents are oriented to this way of life. The more rigid the parents and community are in holding to this way of life, the greater will be the problem of authoritarianism to the youth. Disruption will be greatest where a youth speaks a language that is different from the pattern held by his parents.[18] In situations where parental and church views differ greatly from the youth's views, communication will either break down or be very inadequate. Loyalty on the part of the parents to traditional patterns and adherence to progressive patterns on the part of youth will be a barrier to communication. *The greater the difference, the less the communication.*[19]

For communication to increase or be restored, understanding in relation to points of tension must be developed. *Wholesome communication leads to a sense of security.* Security and consistency develop meaningful values in spite of change. Change can be faced if the proper interpersonal relationships are present. Relationships and communication can be correlated. Where one exists, the other will doubtless be present.

Communication is the result of loving and caring. Much communication is superficial. When tensions arise in family situations or when emotion is at its peak, communication is brought to a minimum. When two persons are speaking, there are really six people involved. For the speaker there is what one says, what one is trying to say, and what one thinks he is saying. For the hearer there are these aspects present: what one hears, what one is trying to hear, and what one thinks he is hearing.

Meaningful communication is the forunner to wholesome relationships. This is a significant factor in developing adequate parent-child, pastor-youth relationships. Youth often feel that their ideas are not considered or even heard; that parents and pastors do not share information which is needed by them. They also feel that pastors and parents are not always sensitive to their needs. Misunderstandings can be reduced on the one hand, and growth toward positive behavior and attitudes can take place on the other, if communication channels remain open.

Youth feel that in times of tension and strained relationships God seems far away. With the improvement of communication and relationships their spiritual situation also improves.[20]

There are a number of factors that lead to the spiritual maturity of youth, of which one is the formal teaching program of the father and the mother. This teaching will be influential to the degree that there are wholesome communication patterns between parents and between parents and youth. [21]

A second factor that influences maturity is the informal or indirect influence of the home. The example of parents' lives is the important factor here. The example will be more readily communicated if it is demonstrated in love and consistency.

A third factor is the parental view of life. If life is merely for living, working, the making of money, and raising the standard of living, religion will have little value and communication will be difficult. With dedication to Christian living where the spiritual emphasis receives first loyalty, communication will be easier.

A fourth factor is the quality of relationships in the home. This factor is most important and will show up in the fabric of every other relationship. *Religious nurture takes place through relationships, and response is the product of meaningful communication.*

When communication breaks down, morale drops and relationships easily become strained. Strained relationships inhibit normal growth in personality and behavior. To experience the best in these areas communication must be kept in high esteem.

Another area of significant relationships is that of child to child within the same family. Lack of affection between children can cause wonder as to whether they are of worth or of sufficient dignity to continue on. The lack of relationships can result in running away from home or even the contemplation of suicide. The following excerpt is one example of child to child rivalry:

> During my childhood, I always had the feeling that I was being picked on. When there was a disagreement, my brothers would usually stick together and I was the only one to argue my point, although at times my younger brother and I joined forces. I don't really know why I felt that way since I was the only girl and I felt kind of alone. . . . One thing that made me feel as if my parents favored my brothers was because when I didn't like to do something or didn't like what was being done, I

would very definitely tell my folks what I thought, whereas my brothers would keep quiet. [22]

This girl felt her rejection was due in some measure to the kind of behavior she exhibited.

Folklore holds that the large family is an ideal environment for the child because he has playmates who are near his own age. He has brothers and sisters to help knock the rough edges off and help him become adjusted to his own group. This, it is felt, will promote unselfishness and other desirable characteristics. [23] Not all these assumptions are well founded. The child from the small family shows ability in choosing his own destiny. He more often plans to continue schooling. If he terminates it, he does so for reasons satisfactory to himself. [24]

It is often the oldest or middle child, not the youngest child, who is most likely to lack proper adjustment. [25] Other factors, such as intelligence, age difference, appearance, personality, parents' attitudes, emotional needs, and personal preferences, are more important than family position alone. [26]

A common response to child to child rivalry is the development of a strong feeling of inferiority. This is the case especially where one child is favored and the unfavored child is made to feel unwanted. [27]

Jealousy is more likely to occur among youth in homes that generate feelings of insecurity. [28] When insecurity is present, children and youth will struggle for the position of least threat. This often brings them into competition for the parents' approval.

Children, even in the same family, differ greatly. They are individuals and must be understood in their own rights. While their needs vary, parents must be certain that they do not show partiality. Each must be treated differently, yet in a similar way.

Parents ought to give ample and equal opportunity for children to develop and pursue fields of vocational interest. Guidance is important, but demands that are contrary to abilities should not be made. Where there are numerous children in the same family, diversification of occupation is desirable and will lead to less competition. Each child should be made to feel that the choice he has made in the area of vocation is significant and worthy of his pursuit. Special care should be given each as they seek God's will for a life of service. *To know His will and to do it is better than competitive motivation.*

ADOLESCENT ASSOCIATIONS

Favorable attitudes toward God and the church are more likely to be held by youth who have parents who have good attitudes, who relate well with their children, who maintain a good teaching program in the home, and who have a good relation to the congregation.

The influence of persons upon persons cannot be minimized. Persons of the same interest, the same drives, and the same desires will exert a considerable amount of influence upon age mates. Youth are pliable. They give a ready ear to individuals who have their concerns at heart. Persons of their own age are the most welcome guides.

It cannot be emphasized too strongly that to become adult members of society, youth must escape from their childish submissive status, must accept and assume responsibility for self-direction, and take their place among their contemporaries. For some youth who have grown up under dominating parents, parents who were overprotective, or parents who without exercising overt authority over them have robbed youth of self-confidence, there may be a problem of achieving an independent state. They may not only be content to remain docile, but may hold fast to their dependent place in a family that gives them security at the cost of further wholesome development. [29]

Love in the family has been praised so much that we forget the price paid by devoted sons and daughters who have been held closely by parents who kept them from growing up as independent adults. [30] It is possible for youth to develop a picture of themselves as unmitigated villains or submissive, docile slaves, developing the feeling of doom to such roles for the rest of their days. [31]

Sometimes it may seem that a youth has forgotten the domestic circle, but his family loyalty has not really weakened. He has simply yielded to broader social experiences beyond the boundaries of the home. [32]

Youth do not want complete freedom. They would not know what to do with it. They may seek release from parental control and family patterns to comply with the often more exciting standards of their own age-group. [33]

The Mennonite adolescent seems to be sensitive about belonging to a minority subgroup. He may, because of this, develop a pattern of fluctuation in his behavior. [34]

Youth's friends become increasingly important as they move into and through adolescence. While friends tend to supplement the home and the school in middle childhood, in adolescence they may take priority over these agencies in their demand for the allegiance of their members. [35] The most potent single influence during youth's development is the power of group approval. Any youth may become a slave to the demands of his group. [36]

In the process of gaining independence some conflict is to be expected. Antagonism and emotional upset can be reduced for parents and youth if both realize that acquiring independence is desirable and necessary. They can do this without losing their parents' love, and they can develop skills which will make it possible for them to assume responsibilities for which their parents now think them incapable. [37]

Older youth often experience a phase of estrangement that may be more bitter than in early adolescence. [38] Money is often a point of contention in the family. The amount of allowance, the use of their earnings for the family's welfare, patterns of spending, using money for tuition for an education, for buying a car, or for recreational purposes are often points of stress. [39] Rebellion against the family is often the result of financial problems. [40]

Youth want to develop a sense of adequacy. They want to be able to take care of their own needs. They move through three stages in arriving at maturity. The first stage is that of dependency. The second is the search for independence. The third is a final leveling off into a wholesome state of interdependence. The struggle to arrive at this third stage is trying, but can be a pilgrimage of joy if understood by both parents and youth and traveled together in understanding relationships.

The peer group relationship also represents a realignment of loyalties. The nature and quality of peer group relationships is a strongly influencing factor in relation to the acceptance of Christian standards. [41] Revolt against parents is often a genuine and necessary act, because parents, unconsciously or otherwise, force the youth to remain dependent and helpless. This may reflect dependency needs and a low level of maturity in parents, causing the developing youth to revolt. Most parents have this need for dependency and it can often result in parent-child conflict. An unhealthy situation can develop where youth accept parental protection without protest. For a person to achieve independence he must become clearly differentiated from his surroundings. Experiences must be provided that help youth to meaningful decision-making and a sense of personal responsibility. They must have experiences that provide clear-cut preferences, responses, feelings, and goals. Youth develop by pitting themselves against others.

The need for "sparring partners" in order to develop individual integrity is the core of the struggle for independence. The first line of opposition is the parents; the second may be the authority figures of the community. The revolt against parental regulations and the practices of the community are not necessarily a rejection of these patterns, but a counter stance against which youth can pit their own process of maturation. The majority of youth accept the authority pattern that society presents. It is this fact that makes the rebellion of youth look less difficult. [42]

A son may rebel against his father's wishes, neither because his father is wrong, nor because his suggestion is off base. A son rebels to gain his independence.

If parents and youth move too far apart, it is possible for a kind of subculture to develop. Although youth mature in the areas of ability for occupation, reproduction, organization, and socialization early, they are still immature in many ways and unable to assume an adult role in society. [43]

If there is not a sound parent-child relationship, youth may be driven to a peer dependency relationship. Sometimes the dependency patterns are so strong that a cessation of the friendship may prove to be a serious crisis. One girl writes:

Then when I was a sophomore I found another girl to be with. We became real close and went everywhere together. Some people teasingly would ask us where our shadow was if we were alone. Our ideas were usually the same and we usually wanted to do the same things at the same time. We both started dating as soon as we were fifteen, but we still were together most of the time because we usually doubled when we had dates. We were so close we wouldn't have much to do with other girls because we thought we could have more fun alone. . . . We are still friends, but there seems to be a sort of wall between us. I miss this friendship because she was one to tell all my troubles to and she understood. [44]

It is interesting to note that this same girl had a very unhappy relationship with her father. She writes:

While in high school, I had some difficulty getting along with Dad. He always thinks he is right and I hate nothing worse than being wrong myself, at least most of the time. . . . Dad would slap me for nothing, back when I was in high school, and this always made me so mad because I thought I was too old to be slapped. [45]

When children come to a certain age, parents may not continue to give them the tenderness and love which they had earlier enjoyed. Not only is it denied, but when they ask for it either directly or indirectly, they are often treated in a fashion that provokes anxiety or pain. As a youth learns that it is not to his advantage to show need for affection, he comes to feel that he is living in a land of enemies. [46]

Dependency relationships with peers of either sex will vary in direct relationship to the degree that the youth feels rejected and unable to communicate with his parents and brothers and sisters.

Identification with peers is increased as a youth feels he must reject his parents' culture in order to become a responsible self. [48]

Peers become a great source of education for youth. A study involving five thousand high-school seniors showed that the greatest amount of sex education came from parents for girls, and from older youth for boys. Magazines and movies also had their influence. The church, Sunday school, and minister rated lowest for both groups as a source of sex education. [49]

The family should provide the kind of context that will educate in many areas for youth's needs. *Proper rapport must be maintained if communication is to continue.*

The family should attempt to make homelife as attractive as possible for the adolescent. The motive for this attraction should not be possessiveness. It is the family's responsibility to help the youth become a self-respecting person capable of making his own decisions. He will have acquired much in the way of personality and values from his parents. However, as he moves out and begins to transfer his loyalty from the parents and the home environment to his peers, he will for the first time be able to become objective about his home and its teaching. [50]

A family that does many things together will want to continue to plan activities that will incorporate the interests of all their youth, insofar as this is possible. Youth may not want to assist in the planning and may reject the activity with a moment's notice. But to stop planning is hardly the answer for a youth who is transferring loyalties. [51]

Youth's struggle for independence is not to be ignored. It is not bad. It is wholesome. It must be understood and guided indirectly. Through the development of independence, youth become responsible adults. They eventually move into a relationship of interdependence, which is the desired result. There seems to be no other route.

The self-picture of the individual is a strong determinant of behavior. This image arises out of youth's spiritual, mental, intellectual, and physical experiences and nature. [52]

The developmental needs of a youth must be understood. His searchings must be directed rather than checked. He is attempting to become a responsible adult in a real world, a world that is new and different. He needs to establish new identities, for in so doing he develops a more meaningful self-concept and pattern of behavior. During this period parents must remain available.

CHURCH AND HOME

If youth are to be nurtured in the Christian way of life, the Christian education program will need to be taken seriously. Both the church and the home will need to teach cooperatively. Inescapable tasks of Christian nurture will need to be faced. There are several of these.[53] Teaching for the future must be weighed against teaching for the present. Much Christian education is future-oriented. The nursery child is prepared for kindergarten. The kindergarten child is prepared for the primary class. This continues on up the ladder. The elementary child is prepared for high school and the high-school graduate for college. This is not only found in Christian education but secular education as well.

This kind of teaching is not adequate for home or church because it bypasses the relevance of education, and its basic task of helping the individual face life in his present context. Teaching must be geared to the level of development for each age. Teaching must help persons face issues where they are now, as well as prepare them for the future.

A second inescapable task of Christian education deals with the teaching of persons to either transmit culture or become an agent of cultural change. It is always the task of the Christian Church to speak to sub-Christian cultural practices of society. It is also the task of the church, under the leadership of the Spirit, to speak prophetically to social issues attempting to bring the judgment of the lordship of Christ to bear upon them. Persons must be taught to retain the significant and important, and to make changes where change could be beneficial to the welfare of the church and its life.

It is not the basic purpose of the church to transmit culture. The word of the Gospel is that which is to be transmitted. The culture may serve only as a vehicle. When it is outdated, depreciated, or useless, it should be discarded. Teaching must be geared, in both home and church, to help individuals relate these two aspects meaningfully. Teaching that does less is less than whole and will form a warped concept in the learning experience of persons. It is less than adequate to have homes assume leadership in finding and pursuing new methods of Christian witness, while the church as a corporate group, represented by its leaders, feels that its unique responsibility is one of restraint and restriction. Both the home and the church must be vitally concerned, and develop a corporate approach to the needs of the gathered and the scattered fellowship.

A third inescapable task in Christian education is that of personal ability as over against grace dependency. It is easy for individuals who have opportunity for training to assume that their contribution in the world is largely the result of personal effort. Training is important, but if it militates against grace dependency, or the power of the Holy Spirit, its efforts will be useless. All persons, in spite of personal ability, feelings of security and adequacy, must come to realize that effort apart from the blessing of God is of little value. Its benefit may have momentary satisfaction, but the eternal quality will be lacking.

These inescapable choices of Christian education lead one to the conclusion that *the home and church are partners in the business of developing Christian persons, and in preparing them for mission.* The task, if viewed as mutual, becomes not only easier but of much more effect.

The home and the church must also enter into communication about basic issues. There must be developing understandings about the basic purposes for the existence of each institution. The final thrust must be a cooperative venture.

American Mennonitism is still sound at the core. It has to a degree recovered its sense of connection with its great past. It has developed a wholesome capacity for self-criticism and an understanding of its own problems and needs. In general, it maintains a good balance of faith and works, inner experience and evangelistic endeavor. There are, however, grave dangers ahead. Fundamentalism must be understood and rejected, as were liberalism and modernism. The doctrines of nonresistance and nonconformity must be restored and made fully relevant to our modern situations. They must not be mere traditions, but must be intelligent, Scripturally grounded convictions. Christian discipleship must become the organizing principle of the Christian faith. The twin, though opposite, problems of traditionalism and worldliness continue to be constant threats. Materialism must be understood for what it is. The home and the church must work together in thinking through the implications of a Christian theology that is both Biblical and relevant. It dare not be a mixture of confusion, but a Christian theology well thought through and personalized in the life and experience of each member of both home and church. [5] [4]

If our youth are to develop basic spiritual conviction and maintain appreciation for the Christian way of life, it must be kept relevant to their basic needs. The church, supported by the home, must plan for teaching that is evaluative in relation to current organization, methods, and materials. Is the present structure adequate? Are there too many agencies and organizations? Does competition saturate the program? Is the church program taken for granted? Is the level of expectancy too low? Many people live and serve as though they don't expect much to happen. When this is the case, little happens. *Results parallel faith.*

Teaching provided by the home and church must also be the kind of teaching that makes people aware of needs. There are individual needs, such as social, spiritual, and mental. There are also group needs, such as those in communication, in fellowship, and in worship. The level of group involvement in both home and church must be raised.

Teaching must make provision for encounter in a living context. *The first mission field is that within the home and the church.* The needs of the total family must be understood and met. The functional approach in teaching must be explored. Simply delivering facts is not sufficient. The material must be made relevant to the learner. Vital issues must be faced. They have been glossed over too long. The problems of recreation, leisure time, Sunday employment, world relationships, social issues, as well as others, need answers that are carefully thought through. Youth are anxious to get on with the business of Christian living. There is not sufficient interest for youth to stay within the confines of the church and struggle over issues that seem irrelevant. They want to move. They desire action and progress within the church or they will go where these are found. Parents and church leaders must provide for learning experiences that face vital issues squarely. *Youth who hold unfavorable attitudes toward the church usually class it as either a low status group, a static group, or a minority group.*

The teaching ministry of home and church must be concerned about relevant experiences. Worship dare not be without form and void. It must be a response to a vital confrontation by the living God. The element of indoctrination in the teaching ministry must **represent an unbiased approach to the Word of God. It will** need to be paralleled by a life of consistency and depth devotion. There will need to be a searching and seeking for the will of God through the living Word of God. The Anabaptist heritage is significant and meaningful, but a careful theology will need to be **thought through for the issues we face of which the Anabaptists probably never dreamed. Christian fellowship will need to be deepened and enriched if youth are to adhere to the church and its program. Fellowship must be centered in a person and not in mere personal interest. It will need to be concerned about functional results. Fellowship that is not related to personal needs will soon deteriorate.** *Fellowship that is not rooted in action will die of want. Christian teaching must regain relevance both to Christ, the church, and to individual needs.*

The teaching provided by both home and church must prepare youth for mission. The gifts of the Holy Spirit will need to be understood and experienced. The Spirit's gifts are diverse. They are given with an awareness of hereditary characteristics. The church must assist persons in the recognition of gifts. Teaching must take place at the point of engagement. The living gift and divine power must merge into action. The experience of spiritual engagement must not be felt only within the context of the church but must reach to youth's own world. Where a living fellowship meets, there God will break forth in power. Teaching must be experienced in the light of personal need and the apparent needs of the individual's personal world. Problems and solutions must be meshed. Man must be understood to be exactly what he is. The living Word must be related to the dying individual.

Teaching must be geared for mission. The gathered family and church must be concerned about the quality of their relationships. The quality of love and relationships within these primary groups will lend a stability that will not be easily shaken in the scattered world.

If home and church are to fulfill their mission, a common enemy[55] *will need to take the place of disorganized threats. When the home and church sense the importance of one mission, a consistency will result which will assist in binding individuals both young and older into a singleness of purpose and mission.*

BROADER DIMENSIONS

Mennonite youth are caught in an intergenerational gap which is accented by changing understandings concerning authority in the home and in the church. In some geographical areas there is strong reaction against authoritarianism. In some locations this came much earlier and in others the present generation is facing it squarely. *Youth react against an authoritarianism which they do not understand.* They are in a hurry to get away from all controls and in the process overlook what is meant by Christian freedom and the source from which it comes. The free person is the person who has freedom to actively follow through on the basis of a commitment that makes a difference in his life. A new understanding of commitment to cause, community, and relationships must be developed, or tragedy may result.

Mennonite youth are also caught in rapid economic changes. There is the problem of materialism, and of a changing occupational pattern. The former ways are not adequate. New methods, means, programs, and plans must be developed. These areas cause youth to be uneasy with the slower action of adults who seem satisfied with the methods and the means of their earlier days. Youth desire, both as a result of their nature and the tension of the current fast-moving economic and social structure, to see action and progress. Many of these areas as well as others tend to cause tensions which must be understood. Parents and church leaders must explore with youth the meaning of change. A careful philosophy of progress needs to be spelled out in the immediate context of problems. Tradition may need to be replaced by new practices. Tradition may have its **place, but when it becomes a leash instead of a ladder,** it should be discarded. *Longevity never guarantees correctness.* Practices that are not Biblical and doctrinal in orientation, that is, according to the fixed truths of God's Word, must constantly be evaluated for their relevance. The concepts of the older generation and the fast-changing concepts of the present generation can easily come into clash. Communication is the immediate approach to the problem. [56]

Persons are multidimensional. At one point a person is sensitive to the traditions of his elders, while at the same time he is open to the influence of his peers. He may also take into account his inner experience as a guiding factor. [57]

Parents and church leaders must be deeply concerned about developing understanding within youth and between youth and adults in relation to the rapid change that is facing the church. One can attempt to shut his eyes, not listen to youth, build barriers, sever communication, and consequently lose them. A better way might be to listen carefully, analyze intelligently, and give sanctified judgment and leadership in relation to the problems all are facing.

A second area of social tension is that of the urban-rural relationship. With the rapid development of many urban areas, the movement of country to city, tensions are inevitable. For a people whose background has been largely agrarian, city life poses many problems.

A large percent of Mennonites who leave the farm for work in the city in nonagricultural pursuits become lost to the Mennonite Church. Urban soil may not be the soil best fitted for the Mennonite Church. It is possibly true that the city soil is too stony, hard, and shallow for Mennonite ideals to take root. The influences of city life have choked out much of the seed sown there. [58] Christ can, however, transform lives anyplace.

Rural society has certain elements of stability which are not present to the same degree in urban life. In the city, differences in social class and wealth create insecurity. [59]

Youth love adventure. At one time they found it through the crusades. At another time, by going west. Today youth find adventure by going to the city. [60]

New and better communities must be built. This is not a call for a superficial, unrealistic, "back-to-the-farm" trend. It is a call to a new and better community pattern. Educational, social, and recreational programs need to be instituted which will raise the cultural level. There is need for a medical program and mutual aid service plus an evangelistic zeal which will make the community truly a center of meaningful Christian discipleship. [61]

The Mennonite community is not functioning as it ought, for perhaps two reasons. Mennonite life may have grown more or less sterile and the impact of contemporary pagan sensate culture may have influenced the Mennonite culture to such a degree as to restrict its effectiveness. [62]

Other studies help us to see that Mennonite youth have many of the same psychological and emotional problems as other youths. Certain problems may be accented among Mennonites because of their relationship to the larger culture and because of the shift among Mennonites from rural to urban residence. [63]

It will be needful for Christian education emphases to give careful guidance in relation to social, spiritual, recreational, and other areas that need constant evaluation and application. During periods of transition, unrest is prevalent. Stable home and church life can be very beneficial in helping individuals make the kind of adjustments that are needful. The trend in mobility makes appropriate and adequate adjustment more difficult. *Teaching for mission in a rapidly changing culture will continue to be a crying need.*

The trend toward urbanization presents a constant challenge to both the home and the church. Urbanization has its effects upon family and homelife. Marriage is not headed for extinction, as some predict, but is rather in a period of transition from a rural to an urban pattern[64] This transition has its influence upon youth. Rejection in farm homes is less likely than rejection in urban homes. [65] The total atmosphere is different. Farm homes tend to retain a more strict and consistent leadership for a greater period of time than city homes. The fact that they are more closely knit tends to lend a greater degree of security in spite of the more authoritarian approach.

While urban homes tend to be less authoritarian, there is also less possibility for a close-knit relationship to emerge. This means that the life found in the urban family must have a high quality to compensate for the lack of constant association.

Rural farm families are often larger than urban families. One reason for this may be the fact that only smaller families are able to be more mobile. Mobility increases one's ability to climb the economic ladder. [66] Academic progress may also be associated with both mobility and urban life. New situations create new tensions. Tensions must be resolved. Both parents and pastors must help youth face the tensions resulting from mobility.

A third area of tension results from the processes of acculturation, assimilation, and secularization. Acculturation is the process of accepting new cultural elements. Assimilation is the acceptance of the basic values which underlie these cultural elements. Secularization means the substitution of profane for sacred values as desirable. [67]

Mennonites now seem to be in the third of a three-stage cycle. They have moved from a community of believers to a community of relatives to a community of individuals. [68] The total social structure emphasizes this trend. In this movement the Mennonite Church has also attempted to maintain the historic culture which they felt was most in keeping with divine sanction. [69] The result has been rapid movement in social and economic areas and slow movement in religious areas. *Broader social acquaintances can assist in making youth more independent, and independence may militate against Christian fellowship.*

Acculturation and assimilation, while dangerous, inasmuch as secularization can result, can also be healthful in that a greater degree of relevance to world need can emerge. Assimilation should be converted to the church's advantage. It could result in a more meaningful contact with the world. The process could be of value in that a broader sense of the meaning of beliefs and practices could develop. The dimensions of love and service can take on new meaning in and through greater world relationships. The Christian fellowship must become the basis of fellowship and nurture for the purpose of strengthening the individuals who find their mission in society at large. The non-Christian group, however, must not become the spiritual basis of operation for even the most wavering member. [70] Both youth and adults who take the mission of the church seriously are subject to these sociological pressures. The church must continually be the resource needed for the members who encounter the living world on its own grounds. *In previous years we have too often either been afraid of or succumbed to the world and its philosophy.*

5 YOUTH ARE CALLED TO BECOME

Youth have needs. Relationship with God has been severed by disobedience. Since the word "disobedience" took on meaning, man has continually been a problem child. The problem is a direct result of personal involvement in a violation of the word and will of the Creator. Persons are in quest of meaning. Behavior manifests a desire for fulfillment, whether it be born of communistic, capitalistic, spiritualistic, naturalistic, pagan, or Christian origin. This quest for meaning seeks fulfillment in ways unbecoming to the kind of creature God intended persons to be. Persons are eternal creatures with unfulfilled needs. They are in quest of a counterpart which will bring to fulfillment their deepest searchings. This apparent emptiness is not a spiritual "given" but an end result of an attempt to pursue the meaning of life in isolation. Persons are in isolation both from their Creator and from their fellow human creatures.

THE REAL PROBLEM

Becoming is a lifelong process, begun at birth. It is facilitated by understanding both one's nature and the process of nurture. We all are the victims of predicament, not of blindness, but of our own choosing. This is a choice each man relives daily. The first parents of the human race set the pattern. This pattern has been clearly followed by all, because through the disobedience of the first family all have been thrown open in a new way to evil. This desire to evil resides within all persons, and they are simply unable to cope with it by themselves. Persons are born babies, not sinners, in the full meaning of the term. In following their evil tendencies they develop into sinful persons. All persons must surrender their vain struggling to the perfection of Jesus Christ, through the experience of faith.

Estrangement from God has been manifest in many ways throughout the course of history. The experiences of history become meaningful to us as we observe a reenactment of the same forces at work in the world, the community, the church, and our homes. The basic human desire of persons is "evil continually." There is something wrong at the heart of each. This fact must be taken into account in the best of our churches and homes. No persons are exempt from the human problem.

Many Mennonite youth appear to have a degree of fluctuation in relation to the way they feel about the Mennonite Church. Many seem to be quite serious about some of the central teachings of the Mennonite Church, such as nonresistance and the showing of love and compassion to all human existence. They desire the church to be relevant, but are not sure that it is. Some feel that there is a great gap between the ethical and moral teachings and the quality of life evident in our homes and churches. Some feel this difference is sufficiently large to justify a critical attitude and nominal relationship to the existing church organization. Others feel that the church is moving too slowly in separating cultural practices from central Biblical truths. [1]

Youth of today have an understanding of the human problem and are painfully aware of separation from God and its implications. They are in search of meaning and notice apparent inconsistencies in the lives of those who by reason of experience should have reached a greater degree of fulfillment. It is estrangement that causes inconsistency in life. The closer the relation of man to God, the greater the degree of consistency in all things.

The basic drive in persons is Godward, yet self-consciousness inhibits full realization of this desire. The present urge is to fulfill the immediate rather than better-known, long-range desires. Youth want to know, they want to become, but are restricted by the forces of iniquity which lay hold of the physical and spiritual self. The spiritual self is made in the image of God and would be more inclined to follow the dictates given were it not for the implications of physical involvement in youth's human pilgrimage.

This pilgrimage throws the youth into competition with his fellows and thus clouds the basic objective which should be clear.

All are prone to evil because of disobedience to righteousness. Sin is a stark reality. It is contrary to the will of God. It hinders each person from becoming the individual God intended. It is actually irrational, and thus is often described as "demonic"; that is, that the one who follows the desire to sin is yielding to the temptations of the evil one. [2]

The Word of God presents persons as creations of great capacity and dignity. All are made in God's image. This is meant to include those attributes of mind and spirit which distinguish man from the animal kingdom. All have the capacity to think God's thoughts after Him. All have a moral nature and conscience. All are aware of the consequences of moral decision-making and the responsibility to God which decisions involve. Thus, having been created in God's image is a glorious fact.

It is possible to go beyond the Bible and make the nature of persons blacker than God has stated. All persons are complex, endowed with many capacities and with great potential. *Any attempt to push the doctrine of human sinfulness so hard as to leave man with no capacity to respond to God's redeeming love is a gross injustice.*

Persons are in need of relationship and relationships. Nurture comes through relating persons both to the God who created them and to their fellowmen. Before nurture can be understood in relationships, several distinct aspects of human depravity must be understood. Depravity makes people self-willed. This runs counter to nurturing relationships. This means that all persons have a struggle with their human nature which leads them to defy the law of God. Sin did not add new desires to human nature, but initiated a revolt of the "flesh" against the "spirit" of man. So the natural self comes into conflict with the spiritual self. [3]

Forgiveness comes through a proper relationship with God and one's fellowmen. Forgiveness is the basic need of persons. Forgiveness is needed, not for being, but for being found in sin. Repentance is a prerequisite to forgiveness. Repentance is basically an attitude, an attitude of sorrow for separation. Wholeness is found in relationships. The Gospel of forgiveness and acceptance must be at work in all church and family relationships. As persons learn to place trust in others and experience acceptance as they are, they begin to understand something of the meaning of the Gospel of forgiveness. Hurts that come through persons are healed best in the context of persons. Through redeemed persons God seeks to reveal His redeeming and healing love. God usually manifests Himself to persons through significant interpersonal relationships. This is not to say that God does not break through confusing interpersonal relationships that may exist, to reach persons. [4]

The previous paragraphs have been an attempt to spell out some of the basic beliefs about persons. These might be summarized as: (1) Persons are created as dependent beings, creatures of purpose in desire of fulfillment; (2) persons are created for relationships with others; (3) persons are neither soul alone nor body alone; (4) persons are a body-soul unity, in defection from the purpose for which they were intended; (5) persons have the potentiality of restoration to wholeness; (6) persons are moral beings responsible for all their choices. [5]

CHRISTIAN AWARENESS

The Scripture very clearly states that parents are to "teach . . . diligently." The implication is that there are truths to be transmitted, and that there is a better way of life.

All persons have needs. The needs spoken to in Scripture are basically spiritual; however, they have implications that reach into the psychological, sociological, and physical realms of life as well. God is concerned for the "wholeness" of persons. He made them. He understands their basic drives, their longings for accomplishment, their thirst for meaning, their intentions, and their failures. These are aspects of "wholeness." God wants persons to understand their needs and have them met.

Even though there is a basic awareness of need, persons must be educated in relation to the dimensions of that need. While the psychological dimension of personality and adjustment may be overdrawn, it must be recognized as having spiritual significance and implications with far-reaching results in Christian nurture.

The central problem of the adolescent is the need to become an increasingly independent and interdependent personality. The implications of this developmental pattern are far-reaching in subsequent years. Children are first very dependent; later they seek to establish a degree of personal identity by becoming independent. Still later the individual in his social context learns that he must become interdependent. Youth cannot live and develop alone. This movement is normal and must be understood and carefully guided rather than ignored or restricted too heavily.

A second need is that of understanding one's own sex and the development of a satisfactory and wholesome relationship with the opposite sex. One's understanding of himself, his personal role in relation to masculine or feminine expectations, and one's adjustment to the same will assist in the development of desirable attitudes. It will also assist in the development of the proper respect for others of the same or of the opposite sex. Personalities can be malformed. Sexual deviations may result from improper self-concepts and unhappy relationships resulting from unwholesome association with parents or friends. For example, *parents may be overprotective, insecure, or inconsistent in their demands and cause much frustration in the life of a youth.*

The third need is for security and a sense of belongingness. Security comes through a sense of personal worth to someone else. Each individual needs someone to love him and believe in him. He develops a sense of security and worth as he estimates his value in relation to others. A youth must never be made to feel that he is rejected or that he does not belong to the family group. While youth's behavior may many times be spoken against, and they may receive punishment for misconduct, they themselves must be shown that they are of worth and that they belong.

The fourth need is that of self-understanding and self-acceptance. Emotional conflicts and emerging moods push a youth toward self-understanding. His abilities will be evaluated. His imperfections will be weighed and in the process a value system of personal worth will emerge. This value system has great influence upon future self-understanding, adjustment to society in general, and upon productivity. This self-understanding grows out of one's family and peer group relationships.

The fifth is a need to develop a wholesome social consciousness, including a clear concept of service and mission. The adolescent must be helped in his movement from self-centeredness to an appreciation of the personalities of other people along with their needs.

The sixth need is that of achieving a consistent and unified concept of life. This need can best be met in a home and church environment where parents and pastors have a clear understanding of the meaning of life and a consistent pattern of operation. [6]

Let us turn next to an area of need not second in nature but of parallel concern. This area of need deals with spiritual dimensions of development for youth. The first is a need for a relevant Christian faith. The adolescent must work through his doubts, and come to the claims of Christ upon his life. For many years he has assumed that the religion of his parents was correct, and no doubt, found it to be satisfying. Now the secondhand religion must become firsthand and in this process there are important issues to be faced. *What may be classed as doubt, lack of faith, or even disbelief may only be the result of examination and exploration, which are both wholesome.* They must, however, be carefully guided. Faith to be meaningful must be relevant to life and its problems. It cannot be passed on and accepted unexplored, and cause significant changes in the self-life. From a Christian perspective nothing has really been learned until it affects the individual in his personal relation to Jesus Christ. [7] In Christian education it is imperative that people be vitally related to the Lord of the church. Religious education may attempt to make people Christian without making them Christians. Christian education is concerned that people become Christians. [8]

A second need is that of coming to terms with one's self-image. With a youth's growing awareness of inadequacies, of failure, and of guilt, it is important that he be brought to a source of healing and security. All need healing. The adolescent must learn this before he can develop an adequate self-concept. This healing comes through proper association with Jesus Christ and the development of a realistic self-image.

A third need is that of developing value guides and ethical convictions. During late adolescence values take on the dimensions of conviction. This means that the value has become a part of the person to the extent that he considers it his own and is willing to allow it to set a pattern for his behavior. The presence of moral and spiritual values is related to self-understanding and self-esteem.

A fourth need is that of creativity in service. Every person has a basic desire to make a lasting contribution. All want to be creative. This urge for creativity needs both stimulation and guidance. It must be channeled into avenues that buttress the Christian faith rather than militate against it. *The value systems of the parents will determine to a large degree the attitude of the child concerning his contribution to life.*

A fifth need is for identification with the Christian Church. This parallels the psychological need to belong. This thirst for fellowship can be met in other groups, but will be met most meaningfully in the context of the church. The church must be a fellowship with high spiritual values, and active in the business of Christian nurture.

With the meeting of psychological and spiritual needs one would expect growth. Growth implies change and one would hope that change would be in the direction of more desirable behavior. The measurement of growth and maturity is difficult. One can only speak of general outcomes that are desirable.

Certain standards can be established to measure the development of spiritual maturity. Even though it is impossible to categorize individual spiritual development according to specific lines of advancement, it is possible to establish some marks against which one may measure progress.

A first general characteristic of spiritual maturity is that of a rich and reflective faith. All youth should be able to distinguish between their earlier childhood faith and their present personal encounter with Jesus Christ. Their faith should be continually expanding, encompassing each issue of life as it emerges.

A second characteristic is that of a dynamic quality concerning the structure of faith. This dynamic power is derived from a growing and meaningful relation to the Word of God and the person of Jesus Christ. It will be characterized by a continual self-surrender, and a knowledge of living as a result of strength derived through the Holy Spirit.

A third characteristic of maturity is a consistency of moral behavior. Long-term goals will replace immediate desires. A personal concern for moral behavior and its consequences will emerge along with concern for one's personal beliefs and their implications.

A fourth dimension of spiritual maturity is that of the development of ability to use constructively both authority and freedom. The maturing person is working through dependency, independency, and interdependency relationships. He recognizes himself as a person, yet in need of relationships. He develops a realistic view of himself and his abilities without feeling strong reactions of inferiority or conceit.

A fifth aspect of maturity is that of possessing a faith that is comprehensive, unified, and integrated. A strand of faith must be woven which becomes relevant to all of life. It must be single-minded and all-inclusive. It must be able to carry the individual through to investment and purpose under the lordship of Christ.

A sixth aspect of maturity is that of development of ability to enter into meaningful relationships with other persons. When a person becomes a new self in Christ, he is drawn into the community of faith: a fellowship of persons with similar experiences, yet different in personality. He will develop the ability to speak the truth in love and self-control, both giving counsel to and taking counsel from his fellows.

A seventh and last aspect of maturity is that of a continual desire for perfection. This perfection is that which is found only in personal encounter with Jesus Christ and in open communication with one's fellowmen. He will be desirous of exploring new spiritual possibilities in light of the answers he has already found satisfying.

God's Word and will are for spiritual movement. This movement is the result of nurture. Nurture should be based upon clear **Biblical concepts and a careful understanding of persons.** God does not choose to work against human nature nor contrary to it. [9] He chooses to work in its context by providing a new nature and indwelling power to bring persons to a new realization of Himself, His will, themselves, and their need.

THE CENTER OF RESPONSIBILITY

If it is the word and will of God that persons become whole, mature, and productive, it then stands to reason that provision must be made through which change can best occur. The Bible speaks in tones that are clearly understood in relation to the Christian home as an educational agent and concerning parental responsibility in family life situations. In the Old Testament, Moses wrote the message of God for the children of Israel, thus: "And these words, which I command thee this day, shall be in thine heart: and thou shalt teach them diligently unto thy children, and shalt talk of them when thou sittest in thine house, and when thou walkest by the way, and when thou liest down, and when thou risest up."[10] In the New Testament, Paul writes to the Ephesians concerning the responsibility of fathers, saying, "And, ye fathers, provoke not your children to wrath; but bring them up in the nurture and admonition of the Lord."[11]

The primacy of the home in religious training must be both admitted and assumed.[12] Family influence is basic for the teaching of religion, and it is the duty of the family to teach by living in fellowship with God. As the growing person experiences a contemporary "incarnation of God," he will assuredly both learn and live accordingly.[13]

The first two or three years of a child's life are most important and determine the trend of personality development.[14] The family is primary in the process of personality development for several reasons: First, it is the primary agent of social influence, and second, it exerts its influence in the most formative years of the child's life. This daily influence is most intense and diffuse, pervading every aspect of the life of the developing child.[15]

It may be necessary to rid ourselves of some concepts that have long been held. For example, that a child is clay in the potter's hands is an imperfect analogy. Clay is completely inert. It yields without protest to the one who is shaping it. It stays put. Children are other than inert and do not stay put. They are possessed by energy which drives them to action whether guided or not. The child has inner urges which the parent cannot prevent. *Parents are not molders in clay but a kind of engineer handling a self-propelling machine of great delicacy that can easily be thrown out of adjustment, but strong enough that only death can stop it.* [16]

Two basic points emerged from a mid-century White House Conference on children and youth. First, that the feelings for children on the part of parents are much more important than the techniques used in training; and second, that the attitude manifest in giving advice to children is much more important than the advice given. [17] Parents create the atmosphere of the home by what they are, and by the quality and degree of relationships which they have established between themselves and their children. [18]

The temptation is always present to feel that the Christian faith can be experienced and transmitted apart from the Christian home. We too easily take family relationships for granted and are not overly concerned as long as the situation is tolerable. Many parents hesitate to attempt to understand the meaning of their relationships and their influence upon personality growth and development. The fast growth of the discipline of psychology as a respectable science that seeks to explain the origin and development of personality must be understood and correlated with the Christian faith and its claims. [19]

Delinquency is not as prevalent where homes exercise inter-personal relationships of high Christian quality. Delinquents are often the result of broken homes, of association with evil companions, or poverty-stricken homes, or of homes with immoral parents. [20]

The Christian family has an inescapable educational function. It is not a school nor a church in a formal sense but has within the nature of its very being a kind of responsibility that cannot be assumed by any other agency nor left to chance.

The Christian family must become a truly Christian human community, sensing its gift and task and sharing in its divine mission. This experience of genuine Christian community in the family prepares each member to become a useful participant in the community of faith, the church. As a youth relates meaningfully to both his family and church, he prepares himself to live in the larger social community where he is called upon to share his life and faith. [21]

A home that does not assume its basic responsibility of providing environment appropriate for wholesome personality development has little purpose for existence. Many homes possess the potential of becoming strong citadels of faith and life but have allowed themselves to give major time to secondary issues. *The basic task of the Christian home is not to "provide" but to "be," for in being one is providing life's greatest essentials.* The family of the twentieth century is marked by instability. It is paying for the independence of its members by the price of its very existence or by an alteration of its form which is beyond its primary purpose. [22]

Most problems in Christian homes do not stem from too little control. The problem rather stems from failure to show adequate love, affection, and respect for personhood. There is often too little psychological space for a child's expanding personality. There is a tendency to resort to strict methods of punishment. Understanding between the parent and child is not what it could be, nor should be. *Psychological scars can be left through the use of "undisciplined discipline" which remain for many years.* Parents must think seriously on the question of what love and nonresistance mean for them in the context of the Christian home. [23]

The Christian Church is a second crucial factor in determining the attitudes, beliefs, and behavior patterns of persons. The pattern of enforcing rules and discipline, the general atmosphere, the interpersonal relationships within the brotherhood and between the leadership and the lay people are highly significant. A person's behavior is often influenced by his degree of identification with and commitment to the church. This is directly related to the type and degree of involvement found for him in the church. [24] Many parents and pastors do not have a clear concept of the church and its basic mission. *It is much easier to fight about the faith than for it.* All church leaders and each parent should attempt to develop a clear understanding of the meaning of the church and its mission in today's world. The church is the body of Christ. Christ is its controlling head. All members together are to constitute a life of unity. Each member is to live under the control of Christ's leadership. The church is the temple of God. It is the habitat of God through the Spirit. Each Christian member becomes a part of this great temple with Christ the head dwelling within him. The church is a brotherhood of believers, united in love for oneness of function.

The church is to be a body separated from the world. The New Testament plainly teaches that the disciples of Christ are to be in the world but not of it. Christians are to wear this world as a loose garment. The church is a disciplinary body. The method of discipline may be more influential than the issue at stake. The church is a suffering body. Full obedience is costly. Grace as revealed in Jesus Christ is not cheap. The lordship of Christ is demanding. The true church is ready to assume its responsibility as a witness to the Gospel. Its total redeemed life is to be a witness of and to the grace and power of God. The church then becomes the final goal of all Christian work.[25] The church is, at the consummation, to represent holiness without blemish. Before the mission of the church can be accomplished in our homes and communities, its basic objective must be clearly understood by all persons involved.

An objective for Christian education has been drawn up by Mennonites for use in helping the church and home fulfill its mission. Its purposes are clearly stated thus:

> Through Christian education the church seeks to help all persons to know God as revealed supremely in Jesus Christ and the Scriptures: to become aware of who they are, of what their situation is, and of their alienation to the end that they may repent of their sin, respond to God's redeeming love in faith, and become members of the body of Christ; to grow in Christ within the community of believers, to walk in the Spirit in every relationship, to fulfill the call to discipleship in the world, and to abide in the Christian hope.[26]

This objective must become a reality in both our homes and our churches if we are to fulfill our call and mission in preparing for and functioning in meaningful witness within the world.

One often gets the impression that the youth problem of today is not one of religion but one of organization and administration. The goal of the Christian Church has become churchmanship rather than sainthood. Churchmanship is too often built upon adherence to a denominational creed rather than the development and integration of moral character. A second weakness of many denominational religious systems is that their religion is demonstrated by a system of narrow and restricted social taboos that have no moral significance outside the narrow religious sect in which they are being practiced.[27] Christians should learn to distinguish between the important and the unimportant. Christians need to learn to take sides, sides that matter and make a difference.

Youth cannot grow properly spiritually on a religion of "don'ts." Real Christianity is not found in adherence to a few aspects of a moral code. The church must be about its business of opening channels of communication so that the transforming power of the Gospel may do its work. At present our reasons for separation seem to be going by default. We must face up realistically to the situation and decide whether or not the principles for which our church fathers suffered and died are an essential part of the Gospel, a secondary matter, or a mistaken idea, no longer relevant to our times.[28] If religion and the church are to meet the needs of educated young people, they must build on rational moral principles and not rely fully on dogma and tradition.[29] Certainly the dogma and tradition may become an essential part of Christian nurture, but we must remember that our basic concern is both material and personal and not material alone. Persons within the church should be related to a small, intimate, face-to-face group. These groups should be person- and need-centered rather than task-centered. Such groups should not be based primarily upon statistical categories but built around developmental tasks. Individuals within these groups should have freedom to make choices within limits set by the larger church fellowship. Communication channels should be kept open between the leaders and the group itself.[30]

Avenues such as these must be explored if the church is to retain and continue to speak to its youth. Christian personality must be developed in the context of true community. This must be a community of faith and mission. The restoration of true community would be a step in the direction of preparing a people for a new outpouring of the Spirit of God. Creative interpersonal relations and unity symbolized by the "loaf" must prevail so that the church may regain and maintain its spiritual vitality and respect among its youth.

Not only do homes and churches assume responsibility in the nurture process, but the individual must be involved as well. The person himself, under God, is the final authority concerning what really takes place within his inner self. The influences of both church and home provide the context through which meaningful decisions can be made. Christianity must be lived in the context of the group, yet it is extremely personal. *Every man lives alone in the context of others, yet he is not truly alone, for the Holy Spirit resides within to breathe form and life into the personal and interpersonal arenas of relationships.*

UTILIZING RESOURCES

Christian nurture is not just a divine imperative but can be divinely guided. God has a plan and a purpose. He does not leave persons alone in their problems but takes them by the hand and says, "This is the way; let us walk in it." God gave to persons the Word as a guideline for activities. The Bible is the great source book of human discipline. Its objective is to build persons into the image of God, to shape and mold life with design and purpose. No one is able to successfully walk alone, nor is it within a person's power to find the way in isolation. All persons need guidelines. The Word serves the purpose of a source book for nurture. The Holy Spirit is its interpreter, and the communion of saints is the ratifying body, who through fellowship must plow the living Word into actual experience.

Lecturing or preaching gives factual knowledge and discussion tends to change behavior. The factual knowledge is necessary before involving discussion can take place. The Christian fellowship is a living context through which behavior can be modified.

A child may practice that which will bring roars of laughter from Daddy, while the same behavior from the same child or from another the following day may merit a slap. The child's concept of his father is immediately threatened. The inconsistency is not easily understood. He shows his rage by slapping his father, which may bring a slap in return. Feelings and attitudes are being built as this kind of activity continues day after day. Many of the problems of children originate with and reside in the parents. *Children must be taught consistency, and this is better caught than legislated.* Children merit praise and appreciation rather than continual blame and discouragement. Some parents find this relationship difficult primarily because they did not receive the same. Praise and appreciation are necessary ingredients for self-respect, confidence, and security.

Children are to render obedience and honor to their parents. *Honor and respect are not legislated.* They come as a result of a kind of life lived before children that naturally produces the same. Honor and respect do not come by the tactic used by one schoolteacher, who upon opening her teaching career said to the class, "Now, children, I hope you will love me." Love is developed in the context of wholesome relationships. Respect is a natural result of esteem. If parents are worthy, the respect is usually present. The human heart responds to love and confidence by honor and respect. To receive honor and respect simply means to be the right kind of person.

The relationship of parents is a large factor in the development of wholesome attitudes and behavior in youth. Our youth are what we make them. Our lives are reflected in theirs.

The Holy Spirit uses the truth of God and Christian relationships to make real and meaningful learning situations. The Holy Spirit is a master teacher. The person, the truth of God, and the living situation are integrated and given perspective at the point of interception by the Spirit. This is nurture. Not only when a person says "I see," but when he is able to take the concept, understanding, or practice, and make it his own, has real learning taken place. The work of the Spirit is to open minds and hearts to the truth and integrate belief and practice. The Spirit does not work counter to psychological developmental tasks, but uses life situations to make learning experiential. The gentle work of the Holy Spirit may be present in a person's soul for years. He may work with him for a long time, but the explosion of new life comes in the middle years when a person has lived long enough to realize the intractability of life, his own great limitations, and the mortality of everything. *When a person discovers that his aspirations and dreams will never realize fulfillment, he finds himself in possession of a vague emptiness, a deep longing that only the Spirit can fill. He searches and finds that at that point Christianity takes on new meaning.* [31] The Holy Spirit can be made a living reality to young people if He is related to all their responsibilities. Curriculum materials must not be "all sweetness and light," if they are to be related in a meaningful way to the nurture process. Curriculum must be built to develop an understanding of life and present it as it is. In addition, it must challenge young people in relation to what they may become through Jesus Christ and the nurture of His Spirit.

The Christian fellowship is also a guideline for Christian nurture. In face-to-face interpersonal relationships both youth and adults find reality in thinking and action. No man lives in isolation. Truth must be tested and lived out in the context of one's fellows. Christian fellowship is more than a pooling of mutual ignorance; it is a relationship with purpose and intent about truths that matter and that make a difference in one's behavior after he leaves the group. Much teaching-learning, so-called, is irrelevant. It does not deal with the basic issues of life. It does not relate the Word to the situation at hand. It becomes superficial. *"Learning is not something done to persons! It is the action of a responsible self experiencing his relationships."* [32] The corporate life of the fellowship must be brought under the discipline of the Holy Spirit. The church must in reality become the fellowship of the forgiven. It must be strong and sensitive, caring for each member. Its concern must also reach to those beyond its bounds. The spirit of the fellowship needs to be corrective and redemptive as it reaches out in love to those both within and beyond the fellowship to proclaim the Gospel of truth. The Christian fellowship, whether in the form of a larger congregation or a small face-to-face group, must ever be on its guard against self-righteousness, complacency, and dead or dying traditionalism. [33] Only in the context of living reality can real nurture take place.

TO BE WHOLE

Ultimately every youth asks himself some basic questions. Who am I? Why am I here? Where am I going? Is there anything worth living for? Is there anything beyond worth my time? To what value system should I give allegiance? Does commitment to Christ solve all problems? The problem can be illustrated by the student who remarked, "Thousands of images and thoughts that flood my mind tire me and I ask for the will to conquer my complexity. I try to give and I have nothing. I try to say 'hope,' but I do not hope. I only endure." Adolescence is a crucial time. It is a time of review and evaluation. The values of his society, church, and home are marched by in review. Many drives are present, but above them all is the drive to find meaning in life. [34]

This prevalent searching plus the inability to measure up to adult standards produces insecurity and guilt feelings. The handling of guilt feelings is one of the early inner needs of youth. The almost intuitive demand to live up to the expectations of others is not met. This failure brings a sense of guilt. *Guilt in the deepest meaning is to feel one's self unworthy of love. Through the imperfect love of parents a child meets the perfect love of God in a partial way.* Out of experiences of parental love or lack of love he develops attitudes about God. One girl, who was afraid of God, confided in her pastor, "When I was small, my mother told me more than once she and Father didn't really want me, for they wanted a boy." This hindered the development of a sense of acceptance by God. Guilt also arises out of failure to meet moral demands placed upon youth by home or church. *Youth's inability to live up even to their own expectations produces guilt.* This guilt feeling can be replaced by knowing that there is a loving God rather than one who stands ready to judge at the slightest digression. [35] Guilt may emerge in the life of a young child because of failure to reach parental standards. While he is safe spiritually, he is growing morally. He needs to understand forgiveness even though he has not as yet realized his inner need. *Forgiveness for acts of sin may be experienced before a child recognizes his sinnerhood and stands ready for the forgiveness and recreating power of God.*

While struggling with guilt and its resultant feelings youth becomes aware of the tangle of dishonesty and make-believe with which many people surround themselves. It would not be so bad if one pretended only to others, but the pretense is also in the light of one's self-concept. Pretending to one's self also encourages pretending to God. [36]

Personal identity for which all youth seek can be greatly lacking. Emotional illness may result. The first step toward the curing of an emotional problem is its recognition. A person who appears to live in a separate world and refuses to face his problem needs special attention. If a youth has a delusion that people are persecuting him, or has such severe "blues" that he is unable to work, he needs understanding care. If he suffers agonies of indecision in making up his mind, or if he experiences moods that swing from depression to exhilaration, these too call for attention. He needs care also if he insists he is ill and medical examination proves otherwise, or if he cannot sleep without medication, is over-irritable, loses interest in his appearance, talks feverishly, skipping from one subject to another, goes on spending sprees beyond his ability, has unfounded fears, or hears or sees things imagined. [37] The healing of emotional illness and restoration to wholeness require training, skill, love, and humility. Sometimes professional help is the only way out and this should be secured without a feeling of humiliation or fear. The wholeness of a personality is at stake.

Personality is a life, unique and understood to be capable of having meaningful experiences. Each personality is a goal-seeking life. Tensions may result from goal-seeking and become rather acute. [38] Some tension is wholesome, but when the tension rises beyond one's threshold of emotional balance, adjustments need to be made. These adjustments, though often attempted, may not prove successful because of either inner conflict or outer tension. *Emotional illness then may become the result of a self in tension. The self one is expected to be and wants to be is placed in tension with the self one understands himself to be.*

Jesus Christ is the answer to tensions. However, sometimes the web is woven so tightly that it is almost impossible for Christ to break through to the inner self. The work of the Spirit in persons through meaningful relationships can be a great asset in breaking down barriers so that Christ can get to the heart of the problem. *To insist that a youth follow Jesus without an adequate understanding of the cause of his tension is merely to drive him to despair.* However, if Jesus could become the inner guest of the soul and live His life over again through his body, things would change. The Christian faith believes that Jesus Christ can adequately do just that. [39] Jesus Christ is able. He is available to meet all needs if He is only given ample opportunity.

Youth must find identity within their context of struggle. Jesus Christ is the complementary dimension of a young person's needs. A youth must learn to identify with Christ, with himself, and with others in his personal and social searchings. The process of learning to know oneself for constructive work is a necessary journey for all youth. [40] A pattern for happiness must be developed in childhood if it is to be experienced by youth. There is a need for exchange with a chum, a friend, or a close relative. This is the need for the most intimate type of exchange in relation to social satisfaction and the development of a sense of security. A sense of loneliness is essential for socialization. Without an awareness of aloneness the social aspect of one's personality would not be properly rounded and shaped. [41]

No man lives by or unto himself. We are part and parcel of the existence of all whom we have met. The title of Ernest Hemingway's *For Whom the Bell Tolls* is taken from a great sermon by John Donne, the Dean of Saint Paul's in London. In this sermon Donne says, "No man is an island intire of it selfe." He belongs to the large "continent"; so we need not ask, "When the bell tolls a death," for whom it is tolling. When it tolls for one it tolls for all, in that we are dependent and related. We are all bound together in the bundle of life and desperately depend upon each other, whether we want to admit it or not. [42] This is no shame, for in depending upon others we learn better how to place confidence in a loving God. It is in the family context that each person begins his experience in these relationships. Through his mother's care the child begins to trust or fear.

Trust is not taught; it is awakened in persons in or through their relationship to others. The trust that a child learns first from mother and later through relationship with father becomes the basis of one's ability to trust God.[43] *Where the parental-child relationships are other than that of trust, the child often rejects the idea of God as being his heavenly Father.* The consistency and stability of parental life in the home is a basic factor in the development of a vital and a meaningful faith in God. Youth expect love from the family and close friends. To be deprived of this love is the deepest hurt one can experience. Hurts such as this may be healed over, but the scars can remain throughout life. These scars leave their impression upon personality and eventually can cause it to become impenetrable. This kind of scar is not the kind that will merit credit on the day of judgment. Each scar will be a witness against parents and friends in relation to the unchristian attitudes and actions that were inconsiderate of impressionable lives being shaped for eternity.

Parents need a renewed sense of urgency about their chief business. It is to provide the kind of atmosphere that will allow for wholesome personhood in an environment of warmth and security. Healthy interpersonal relationships and an attitude of loving forgiveness must prevail. *It should never be beyond a parent to seek forgiveness from a child if a wrong has happened as a result of poor parental judgment.* This will cultivate a sense of warmth and a desire within the child to seek forgiveness when needed. No parent who confesses his failures, unworthiness, and inability loses respect with family members in the context of loving forgiveness. When persons in family relationships are able to experience the healing power of forgiveness, the road to the forgiveness of God becomes more realistic and much more readily traveled.

Persons thirst for meaning in life. It is daily sought, but found only as one is able to develop a sense of worth and dignity in the context of his relationships with himself and his friends, and also with God. Parents must move from the realm of "telling" and begin to practice with greater zeal the meaning of a consistent life of faithful Christian living.

Christian nurture is a lifelong experience. It should be rooted in the grace of God and watered daily by His Word in the context of dynamic and wholesome interpersonal relationships in both the home, the church, and the community. The quality of learning experiences is deeply significant. For example, it is not as important to have family worship daily as it is to practice carefully the truth taught in one meaningful, weekly family worship experience. Meaningful nurture is influenced more by relationships than by content. The pastor may have a powerful and meaningful sermon in words, but if his life does not correspond with the truth taught, his nurture score is embarrassing.

Youth are nurtured more by what leaders are than by what they say. Christian parents, pastors, and other youth leaders must rise up and do, before speaking so freely, so that when something is said it will be charged with living reality. Only then has real teaching taken place.

THE END

UNRESOLVED ISSUES

While many problem areas were explored in these pages many issues remain for further study. The Christian Nurture Study Committee feels that a remaining problem is the challenge of more adequately defining a "model youth."

The question of the causes for youth deviancy needs further exploration. Are the freewill choices of youth to be placed on the same level as developmental factors, such as frustrations, unhappiness, and anxiety, for example?

Is the lack of faith and the presence of doubt an inevitable experience of adolescence?

Are there any legitimate outlets for adolescent hostility?

Are conversion and emotional development related? If so, in what way or ways?

Is a well-adjusted youth one who accepts the teachings of home and church without question?

What is the relation between freedom and commitment, and what is meant by authority?

The nature and authority of the Biblical church along with participation in its program for adolescents need to be spelled out more carefully. The meaning of church membership for the adolescent seems to need clarification.

These are but a few of the unresolved issues that call for careful attention.

WHERE TO BEGIN

Pastors will need to take the task that has been placed upon them more seriously. Greater effort should be demonstrated in:

1. Attempting to understand persons.
2. Working with people rather than rule books.
3. Keeping abreast of youth's moods, temptations, needs, and possibilities.
4. Opening oneself for counsel. This will call for greater association with youth and the establishing of rapport.
5. Praying both for and with youth.

Parents will need to stop and reevaluate their responsibilities in the light of the current needs. They must attempt to:

1. Communicate more clearly with youth.
2. Accept all youth without respect.
3. Practice a more consistent life.
4. Understand the role and nature of various kinds of discipline.
5. Demonstrate love and major in daily Christian living.

Youth are not exempt, for they must work hard to:

1. Understand themselves and their pastors and parents.
2. Seek to commit themselves to the lordship of Jesus Christ.
3. Take advantage of opportunities to grow in Christian faith and practice.
4. Choose Christian associates.
5. Seek the will of God in all relationships.

Discussion groups of pastors, parents, and youth could be planned which would use the contents of these chapters for sharing. This could help much in arriving at an understanding of the challenge of maturing.

1. Small prayer cells could meet for sharing on vital issues related to nurture.
2. Parent groups could discuss problems they face with teen-agers.
3. Youth could meet to discuss the meaning of Christian commitment.
4. Pastors could preach on areas of concern related to nurture in the home and the church.
5. Youth leaders could open themselves for counsel to youth.

CONCLUSION

While the topic of Christian nurture was not approached from every angle that should be represented, there was an attempt to look at basic issues in the nurture process. An effort was made to explore and consolidate the concerns of the Christian Nurture Study Committee of the Mennonite Church. Much credit must go to them, and to many others for available research materials on the subject. Throughout these chapters an attempt was made to consolidate the thinking of many persons on the issues of concern.

An attempt was made to identify basic factors in the nurture of youth. It is clearly understood that there are yet many unresolved issues and numerous areas in need of additional study. While the limitations of both time and ability have curtailed a more comprehensive study, it is hoped that the basic insights discussed herein might give needed help in rearing our young people for Christ and the church.

It seems very evident that a Christian environment, where love and understanding relationships are present, is the most appropriate for the nurture of youth. This means that the basic pursuit of life is spiritual and not material. *Children tend to become what their parents are. It is therefore important that parents live the kind of life that they want perpetuated.*

Christian values must be understood and developed in youth. Parents must be concerned about the kind of home atmosphere demonstrated. They will need to know how to relate meaningfully as parents both to each other and to the children. Careful guidance must be given to youth in decision-making in all areas of life. Christian vocations must be understood and encouraged along with a deeper sense of the lordship of Christ in every life pursuit.

It is hoped that the glory might go to God for any help received through the contents of these chapters. The greatest tribute of appreciation would be the realization that the church, the home, and individual youth have been influenced for God and for good in their pursuit of the meaning of life and its mission. It is hoped that many youth might answer the call to become genuine Christian personalities.

FOOTNOTES

CHAPTER 1

1. Calvin Redekop, "Mennonite Youth Self Reports" (unpublished paper), p. 3.

2. *Ibid.,* p. 3.

3. Ruth Z. Martin, "Factors Affecting Emotional Adjustment in Mennonite Teenagers" (unpublished paper, Goshen College, Goshen, Indana, 1957), p. 42.

4. Calvin Redekop, *op. cit.,* p. 7.

5. Lester Glick, "The Explication and Prediction of the Concept Adjustment" (unpublished paper), p. 7.

6. Christian Nurture Study Committee, "Summary and Conclusions" (unpublished paper), p. 30.

7. Orval Shoemaker, "Mennonite Family Problems and Needs Which Should Concern Us, as Seen by a Social Worker" (unpublished paper), p. 2.

8. Calvin Redekop, "Areas of Adolescent-Parent Tension" (unpublished paper), pp. 1-5.

9. Calvin Redekop, "A Working Paper on Adolescence" (unpublished paper), p. 16.

10. J. M. Hunt, ed., *Personality and the Behavior Disorders,* Vol. II (New York: The Ronald Press Co., 1946), p. 711.

11. Ruth Strang, *The Adolescent Views Himself* (New York: McGraw-Hill Book Co., Inc., 1957), pp. 377 f.

12. *Ibid.,* p. 376.

13. Paul E. Johnson, *Personality and Religion* (New York: Abingdon Press, 1957), p. 183.

14. Rudolph M. Wittenburg, *Adolescence and Discipline* (New York: Association Press, 1959), p. 53.

15. Urie A. Bender, "The Moral and Spiritual Status of Mennonite Youth" (unpublished paper), pp. 3-4.

16. Nurture Study Committee, *op. cit.,* p. 26.

17. Calvin Redekop, "A Working Paper on Adolescence," pp. 22-24.

18. Christian Nurture Study Committee, "Analysis of the Problem" (unpublished paper), p. 21.

19. Rudolph M. Wittenburg, *op. cit.,* p. 117.

20. Paul E. Johnson, *op. cit.,* p. 188.

21. *Ibid.,* p. 188.

22. Calvin S. Hall and Gardner Lindzey, *Theories of Personality* (New York: John Wiley and Sons, Inc., 1957), p. 128.

23. Carl F. H. Henry, "Christian Education and the World of Culture," *Mennonite Quarterly Review* (1958), Vol. XXXII, p. 309.

24. Atlee Beechy, "Students: A Psychological Interpretation" (unpublished paper), pp. 3 f.

25. Lloyd L. Ramseyer, "Christian Nonconformity in a Conformist Age," *Mennonite Quarterly Review* (1959) Vol. XXXIII, p. 342.

26. *Ibid.,* p. 343.

27. Carol Larson, *Church Participation and Social Adjustment of High School and College Youth,* Washington Agriculture Experiment Stations Institute of Agricultural Sciences, State College of Washington (Bulletin 550, May, 1954), pp. 23 f.

28. Ray Horst, "Youth Problems as Related to Family Experiences as Seen Through the VS and I-W Program" (unpublished paper), p. 6.

29. Guy Hershberger, "Suggestions for Improving the Small Christian Community," *Proceedings of the First Conference on Mennonite Cultural Problems* (North Newton, Kansas: The Bethel Colege Press, 1942), p. 59.

30. Paul E. Johnson, *op. cit.,* p. 158.

CHAPTER 2

1. John 3:3.

2. II Corinthians 5:17.

3. Christian Nurture Study Committee, "Analysis of the Problem" (unpublished paper), p. 23.

4. J. C. Wenger, "What Christ Can Do for Youth" (unpublished paper), p. 6.

5. *Ibid.*, pp. 7 f.

6. Philippians 3:14.

7. J. C. Wenger, "The Ideal Youth" (unpublished paper), *passim.*

8. Lester Glick, "An Explication and Prediction of the Concept Adjustment" (unpublished paper), *passim.*

9. Urie A. Bender, "The Moral and Spiritual Status of Mennonite Youth" (unpublished paper), p. 4.

10. Wayne E. Oates, *The Religious Dimensions of Personality* (New York: Association Press), p. 269.

11. Lawrence M. Bixler, *The Role of Christian Parents in Influencing Emotional Maturity in Their Children* (Fort Worth: Southwestern Baptist Theological Seminary; unpublished doctoral dissertation, 1958), p. 74.

12. *Ibid.*, p. 75.

13. Dorwin Cartwright, "Human Relations," Vol. IV, No. 4, 1951.

14. Ray Horst, "Youth Problems as Related to Family Experiences as Seen Through the VS and I-W Program" (unpublished paper), pp. 3 f.

15. Rudolph M. Wittenburg, *Adolescence and Discipline* (New York: Association Press, 1959), pp. 211 f.

16. *Ibid.*, pp. 17 f.

17. Paul E. Johnson, *Personality and Religion* (New York: Abingdon Press, 1957), p. 155.

18. *Ibid.*, pp. 155 f.

19. Ivan Nye, *Family Relationships and Delinquent Behavior* (New York: John Wiley and Sons, Inc., 1958), p. 71.

20. *Ibid.*, p. 71.

21. Carol Larson Stone, *Church Participation and Social Adjustment of High School and College Youth,* Washington Agriculture Experiment Stations Institute of Agricultural Sciences, State College of Washington (Bulletin 550, May, 1954), p. 1.

22. Romans 10:17.

23. Harold E. Bauman, "The Spiritual Maturity of Goshen College Mennonite Freshmen" (unpublished thesis summary), p. 5.

24. Paul H. Landis, *Adolescence and Youth, The Process of Maturing* (New York: McGraw-Hill Book Co., Inc., 1952), p. 170.

25. Arnold Gesell, Frances Ilg, and Lois Bates Ames, *Youth, The Years from Ten to Sixteen* (New York: Harper and Brothers, Publishers, 1956), p. 273.

26. Louis Linn, Leo Schwartz, *Psychiatry and Religious Experience* (New York: Random House, 1958), p. 49.

27. Calvin Redekop, "Mennonite Youth Self Reports" (unpublished paper), pp. 4 f.

28. Carl F. H. Henry, "Christian Education and the World of Culture," *Mennonite Quarterly Review* (1958), Vol. XXXII, p. 313.

29. Paul E. Johnson, *op. cit.*, p. 222.

30. Paul Friesen Barkman, "A Study of the Relationships of the Need for Belonging and Conformity to Religious Beliefs and Values in a Christian College" (unpublished PhD thesis, New York University, 1959), pp. 133 f.

31. Fritz Heider, *The Psychology of Interpersonal Relations* (New York: John Wiley and Sons, Inc., 1958), p. 173.

32. Paul Tournier, *The Whole Person in a Broken World* (New York: Harper and Row, Publishers, 1964), pp. 13 f.

33. *Ibid.*, p. 12.

34. Robert A. Raines, *New Life in the Church* (New York: Harper and Row, Publishers, 1961), p. 42.

35. *Ibid.*, p. 42.

36. Atlee Beechy, "Preliminary Report of the Mennonite Youth Fellowship Study" (unpublished paper), *passim.*

37. Harold E. Bauman, *op. cit.*, p. 6.

38. Christian Nurture Study Committee, "Summary and Conclusions" (unpublished paper), p. 30.

39. *Ibid.*, p. 28.

40. Reuel Howe, *The Creative Years* (Greenwich: The Seabury Press, 1959), pp. 198-209.

CHAPTER 3

1. Harold E. Bauman, "Family Factors in the Development of Spiritual Maturity" (unpublished paper), p. 9.

2. *Ibid.*, p. 9.

3. Gibson Winters, *Love and Conflict: New Patterns in Family Life* (New York: Doubleday and Co., 1958), p. 125.

4. Paul E. Johnson, *Personality and Religion* (New York: Abingdon Press, 1957), p. 185.

5. Paul H. Landis, *Social Control* (New York: J. B. Lippincott Company, 1939), p. 70.

6. Calvin Redekop, "Mennonite Youth Self Reports" (unpublished paper), p. 7.

7. *Ibid.*, p. 16.

8. *Ibid.*, p. 18.

9. *Ibid.*, p. 19.

10. Christian Nurture Study Committee, "Summary and Conclusions" (unpublished paper), pp. 27 f.

11. C. Henry Smith, "Mennonites and Culture," *Mennonite Quarterly Review,* (1938), Vol. XXII, p. 84.

12. Raymond G. Kuhlen and George G. Thompson, ed., *Psychological Studies of Human Development* (New York: Appleton-Century-Crafts, Inc., 1952), p. 386.

13. J. McV. Hunt, ed., *Personality and the Behavior Disorders,* Vol. II (New York: The Ronald Press Company, 1944), p. 695.

14. Paul H. Landis, *op. cit.*, p. 74.

15. Atlee Beechy, "Students: A Psychological Interpretation" (unpublished paper), pp. 2 f.

16. J. Howard Kauffman, "A Comparative Study of Traditional and Emergent Family Types Among Midwest Mennonites" (unpublished doctoral dissertation, University of Chicago, 1959), pp. 177 f.

17. Christian Nurture Study Committee, *op. cit.*, pp. 28 f.

18. Marion J. Radke, *The Relation of Parental Authority to Children's Behavior and Attitudes* (Minneapolis: The University of Minnesota Press, 1946), p. 2.

19. Kuhlen and Thompson, *op. cit.*, p. 385.

20. F. Ivan Nye, *Family Relationships and Delinquent Behavior* (New York: John Wiley and Sons, Inc., 1958), p. 83.

21. Rudolph M. Wittenburg, *Adolescence and Discipline* (New York: Association Press, 1959), p. 107.

22. *Ibid.*, p. 167.

23. *Ibid.*, p. 168.

24. Ernest M. Ligon, *Dimensions of Character* (New York: The Macmillan Company, 1956), p. 109.

25. Floyd M. Martinson, *Marriage and the American Ideal* (New York: Dodd, Mead, and Co., 1960), p. 447.

26. Christian Nurture Study Committee, *op, cit.,* pp. 26 f.

27. Christian Nurture Study Committee, "Analysis of the Problem" (unpublished paper), p. 17.

28. Harold E. Bauman, *op. cit.*, p. 6.

29. Ray Horst, "Youth Problems as Related to Family Experiences as Seen Through the VS and I-W Program" (unpublished paper), pp. 2 f.

30. Calvin Redekop, *op. cit.*, p. 203.

31. Mary Royer, "Maximizing the Family Worship Experience for Children" (unpublished paper), p. 2.

32. Hadley Contril, "The Intensity of an Attitude," *Journal of Abnormal and Social Psychology,* Vol. XLI, 1946, pp. 129-35.

33. Norman Loux, "Family Factors in Development of Personality Problems" (unpublished paper), p. 4.

34. Gordon W. Allport, *The Nature of Prejudice* (Boston: The Beacon Press, 1954), p. 31.

35. *Ibid.*, pp. 395 f.

36. *Ibid.*, p. 396.

37. *Ibid.*, p. 403.

38. *Ibid.*, p. 404.

39. *Ibid.*, p. 407.

40. *Ibid.*, p. 428.

41. *Ibid.*, p. 435.

42. *Ibid.*, p. 440.

43. *Ibid.*, p. 445.

44. *Ibid.*, p. 446.

45. *Ibid.*, p. 456.

46. Paul E. Johnson, *op. cit.*, p. 190.

47. *Ibid.*, p. 190.

48. Donald Snygg and Arthur W. Combs, *Individual Behavior* (New York: Harper and Brothers, Publishers, 1949), p. 8.

49. *Ibid.*, p. 12.

50. *Ibid.*, p. 22.

51. J. Howard Kauffman, "Mennonite Family Patterns and Youth Deviancy, A Theoretical Analysis" (unpublished paper), pp. 18 f.

52. Lawrence M. Bixler, *The Role of Christian Parents in Influencing Emotional Maturity in Their Children* (Fortworth: Southwestern Baptist Theological Seminary; unpublished doctoral dissertation, 1958), p. 70.

53. J. Howard Kauffman, "Mennonite Family Trends and Their Significance" (unpublished paper), pp. 11-13.

54. Robert F. Winch, "The Study of Personality in the Family Setting," *Social Forces* (1950), Vol. XXVIII, pp. 314 f.

55. Percival M. Symonds, *The Dynamics of Parent-Child Relationships* (New York: Bureau of Publications, Teacher's College, Columbia University, 1949), p. 165.

56. *Ibid.*, p. 5.

57. Carl R. Rogers, *Client-Centered Therapy* (Boston: Houghton-Mifflin Company, 1951), p. 381.

58. Christian Nurture Study Committee, "Summary and Conclusions" (unpublished paper), p. 30.

59. *Ibid.*, p. 26.

60. Rogers, *op. cit.*, pp. 348-59.

61. Ruth Strang, *The Adolescent Views Himself* (New York: McGraw-Hill Book Co., Inc., 1957), p. 361.

62. *Ibid.*, p. 363.

63. John Andrew Hostetler, *The Sociology of Mennonite Evangelism* (Scottdale, Pennsylvania: Herald Press, 1954), p. 261.

64. Christian Nurture Study Committee, *op. cit.*, p. 30.

65. *Ibid.*, p. 29.

66. *Ibid.*, p. 29.

67. *Ibid.*, pp. 29 f.

68. Harold E. Bauman, "The Spiritual Maturity of Goshen College Mennonite Freshmen" (unpublished thesis summary), p. 5.

69. Calvin Redekop, *op. cit.*, p. 13.

CHAPTER 4

1. Christian Nurture Study Committee, "Analysis of the Problem" (unpublished paper), p. 18.

2. *Ibid.*, p. 18.

3. Robert J. Havighurst, *Human Development and Education* (New York: Longmans, Green and Co., 1953), p. 120.

4. Christian Nurture Study Committee, *op. cit.*, p. 18.

5. Nathan W. Shock, "Some Physiological Aspects of Adolescence," in Jerome M. Seidman, *The Adolescent, A Book of Readings* (New York: Henry Holt, 1953), p. 118.

6. Calvin Redekop, "A Working Paper on Adolescence" (unpublished paper), p. 2.

7. *Ibid.*, pp. 2 f.

8. Alexander Frazier and Lorenzo K. Lesonbee, "Adolescent Concerns with Physique," in Jerome M. Seidman, *op cit.*, p. 140.

9. Calvin Redekop, *op. cit.*, p. 5.

10. Christian Nurture Study Committee, *op. cit.*, p. 14.

11. Calvin Redekop, *op. cit.*, p. 3.

12. Harold E. Jones, "Adolescence in Our Society," In Jerome M. Seidman, *op. cit.*, p. 57.

13. Robert Winch, "The Study of Personality in the Family Setting," *Social Forces* (1950), Vol. XXVIII, pp. 312 f.

14. Christian Nurture Study Committee, *op. cit.*, p. 19.

15. Paul H. Landis, *Adolescence and Youth, The Process of Maturing* (New York: McGraw-Hill Book Co., Inc., 1952) p. 150.

16. *Ibid.*, p. 150.

17. J. Howard Kauffman, "A Comparative Study of Traditional and Emergent Family Types Among Midwest Mennonites" (unpublished doctoral dissertation, University of Chicago, 1959), p. 176.

18. Calvin Redekop, "Areas of Adolescent-Parent Tension" (unpublished paper), p. 8.

19. Christian Nurture Study Committee, "Summary and Conclusions" (unpublished paper), p.32.

20. Harold E. Bauman, "The Spiritual Maturity of Goshen College Mennonite Freshmen" (unpublished thesis summary), p. 10.

21. Harold E. Bauman, "Family Factors in the Development of Spiritual Maturity" (unpublished paper), pp. 4-6.

22. Calvin Redekop, "Mennonite Youth Self Reports" (unpublished paper), p. 4.

23. Paul H. Landis, *Teenage Adjustments in Large and Small Families,* Washington Agriculture Experiment Stations Institute of Agricultural Sciences, State College of Washington (Bulletin 549, April, 1954), p. 18.

24. *Ibid.*, p. 22.

25. Ruth Strang, *The Adolescent Views Himself* (New York: McGraw-Hill Book Co., Inc., 1957), p. 371.

26. *Ibid.*, p. 371.

27. Percival M. Symonds, *The Dynamics of Parent-Child Relationships* (New York: Bureau of Publications, Teacher's College, Columbia University, 1949), p. 102.

28. Raymond G. Kuhlen and George G. Thompson, ed., *Psychological Studies of Human Development* (New York: Appleton-Century-Crafts, Inc., 1952), p. 367.

29. Lawrence K. Frank, "The Adolescent and the Family," *Adolescence,* 43rd Yearbook, Part 1, National Society for the Study of Education. (Chicago: University of Chicago Press, 1944), p. 247.

30. *Ibid.*, p. 248.

31. *Ibid.*, p. 251.

32. Arnold Gesell, Frances Ilg, and Lois Bates Ames, *Youth, The Years from Ten to Sixteen* (New York: Harper and Brothers, Publishers, 1956), p. 252.

33. Lawrence K. Frank, *op. cit.*, p. 247.

34. Christian Nurture Study Committee, *op. cit.*, p. 28.

35. Robert J. Havighurst, *op. cit.*, p. 111.

36. *Ibid.*, p. 112.

37. Ruth Strang, *op. cit.*, p. 396.

38. *Ibid.*, p. 357.

39. *Ibid.*, pp. 357 f.

40. *Ibid.*, p. 357.

41. Christian Nurture Study Committee, *op. cit.*, p. 27.

42. Calvin Redekop, "A Working Paper on Adolescence," pp. 9 f.

43. *Ibid.*, p. 10.

44. Calvin Redekop, "Mennonite Youth Self Reports," p. 5.

45. *Ibid.*, p. 5.

46. Paul E. Johnson, *Personality and Religion* (New York: Abingdon Press, 1957), pp. 184 f.

47. Calvin Redekop, "Areas of Adolescent-Parent Tension" (unpublished paper), p. 8.

48. *Ibid.*, p. 8.

49. Floyd M. Martinson, *Marriage and the American Ideal* (New York: Dodd, Mead, and Co., 1960), p. 420.

50. *Ibid.*, p. 425.

51. *Ibid.*, p. 425.

52. Christian Nurture Study Committee, *op cit.*, p. 28.

53. David Hunter, *Christian Education as Engagement* (New York: Seabury Press, 1963), *passim*.

54. Harold S. Bender, "Outside Influences on Mennonite Thought," *Proceedings of the Ninth Conference on Mennonite Educational and Cultural Problems* (North Newton, Kansas: The Mennonite Press, 1953), pp. 33-41.

55. Gordon W. Allport, *The Nature of Prejudice* (Boston: The Beacon Press, 1954), p. 41.

56. Atlee Beechy, "The Contemporary Mennonite Student" (unpublished paper), pp. 4 f.

57. Paul E. Johnson, *op. cit.*, p. 156.

58. J. Winfield Fretz, "Mennonites and Their Economic Problems," *Mennonite Quarterly Review* (1940), p. 199.

59. Guy F. Hershberger, "Appreciating the Mennonite Community," *The Mennonite Community* (January, 1947), p.6.

60. *Ibid.*, p. 7.

61. *Ibid.*, p. 7.

62. Guy F. Hershberger, "Suggestions for Improving the Small Christian Community," *Proceedings of the First Conference on Mennonite Cultural Problems* (North Newton, Kansas: The Bethel College Press, 1942), p. 53.

63. Christian Nurture Study Committee, *op. cit.*, p. 26.

64. Ernest W. Burgess and Paul Wallin, *Engagement and Marriage* (New York: J. B. Lippincott Company, 1953), p.31.

65. Douldner, "The Basic Personality Structure and the Sub-group," *The Journal of Abnormal and Social Psychology* (1946), Vol. 41, p. 357.

66. Paul H. Landis, *Teenage Adjustments in Large and Small Families,* Washington Agriculture Experiment Stations Institute of Agricultural Sciences, State College of Washington (Bulletin 549, April, 1954), p. 13.

67. Calvin Redekop, "Patterns of Cultural Assimilation Among the Mennonites," *Proceedings of the Eleventh Conference on Mennonite Educational and Cultural Problems* (North Newton, Kansas: The Mennonite Press, 1957), p. 101.

68. *Ibid.*, p. 104.

69. *Ibid.*, pp. 100 f.

70. *Ibid.*, p. 109.

CHAPTER 5

1. Atlee Beechy, "The Contemporary Mennonite Student" (unpublished paper), p. 3.

2. Christian Nurture Study Committee, "Analysis of the Problem" (unpublished paper), p. 21.

3. J. C. Wenger, "What Christ Can Do for Youth" (unpublished paper), p. 1.

4. Harold E. Bauman, "Family Factors in the Development of Spiritual Maturity" (unpublished paper), p. 9.

5. W. Norman Pittenger, *The Christian Understanding of Human Nature* (Philadelphia: The Westminster Press, 1964), pp. 18-21.

6. Harold E. Bauman, "The Spiritual Maturity of Goshen College Mennonite Freshmen" (unpublished thesis summary), *passim.*

7. Howard Grimes, *The Church Redemptive* (Abingdon Press, 1958), p. 93.

8. Robert A. Raines, *New Life in the Church* (New York: Harper and Row, 1961), pp. 26 f.

9. J. C. Wenger, *op. cit.*, p. 2.

10. Deuteronomy 6:6, 7.

11. Ephesians 6:4.

12. Alta Mae Erb, "An Ideal Pattern for a Christian Home of Today," *Proceedings of the Sixth Annual Conference on Mennonite Cultural Problems* (North Newton, Kansas: The Bethel College Press, 1947), pp. 87-94.

13. Wesner Fallaw, "How the Family Teaches Religion," *Religious Education,* Vol. XLIII, 1948, pp. 3-6.

14. Ray E. Baber, *Marriage and the Family* (New York: McGraw-Hill Book Co., 1953), pp. 254 f.

15. J. Howard Kauffman, "Mennonite Family Patterns and Youth Deviancy, A Theoretical Analysis" (unpublished paper), p. 9.

16. Ray E. Baber, *op. cit.*, p. 255.

17. *Ibid.*, p. 304.

18. J. C. Wenger, "Biblical Standards for Parent-Child Relationships" (unpublished paper), p. 5.

19. Harold E. Bauman, "Family Factors in the Development of Spiritual Maturity" (unpublished paper), p. 1.

20. Donald Snygg and Arthur W. Combs, *Individual Behavior* (New York: Harper and Brothers, Publishers, 1949), p. 6.

21. Christian Nurture Study Committee, *op. cit.*, p. 24.

22. Willystine Goodsell, *A History of Marriage and the Family* (Revised Edition, New York: The Macmillan Co., 1934), p. 482.

23. Christian Nurture Study Committee, "Summary and Conclusions" (unpublished paper), p. 32.

24. *Ibid.*, p. 27.

25. H. S. Bender, "The Mennonite Conception of the Church and Its Relation to Community Building," *Mennonite Quarterly Review* (1945), Vol. XIX. pp. 90-100.

26. Christian Education Seminar, "Objective," North Newton, Kansas, 1963.

27. Paul H. Landis, *Adolescence and Youth, The Process of Maturing* (New York: McGraw-Hill Book Co., Inc., 1952), pp. 179-85.

28. Lloyd L. Ramseyer, "Christian Nonconformity in a Conformist Age," *Mennonite Quarterly Review* (1959), Vol. XXXIII, p. 342.

29. Paul H. Landis, *op. cit.*, p. 185.

30. Paul B. Maves (ed.), *The Church and Mental Health* (New York: Charles Scribner's Sons, 1953), pp. 94-96.

31. Robert A. Raines, *op. cit.*, p. 28.

32. Robert R. Boelke, *Theories of Learning in Christian Education* (Philadelphia: The Westminster Press, 1962), p. 26.

33. Christian Nurture Study Committee, *op. cit.*, p. 31.

34. Atlee Beechy, "Students: A Psychological Interpretation" (unpublished paper), p. 3.

35. Harold E. Bauman, "The Claim of Christ on Youth" (unpublished paper), pp. 1 f.

36. John Baillie, *Invitation to Pilgrimage* (New York: Charles Scribner's Sons, 1942), p. 20.

37. Delmar Stahly, C. J. Rempel, John R. Schmidt, C. Krahn, and others, "Mennonites and Mental Health," *Mennonite Life,* North Newton, Kansas. Vol. XIX (1954), pp. 133-43.

38. Paul E. Johnson, *Personality and Religion* (New York: Abingdon Press, 1957), p. 239.

39. Culbert G. Rutenber, *The Price and the Prize* (Philadelphia: The Judson Press, 1953), p. 99.

40. Atlee Beechy, *op. cit.*, p. 3.

41. Harry Stack Sullivan, *Interpersonal Theory of Psychiatry* (New York: Norton, 1953), p. 261.

42. W. Norman Pittenger, *op. cit.*, p. 34.

43. Harold E. Bauman, "Family Factors in the Development of Spiritual Maturity," p. 7.